Mirror of the Heart

MIRROR OF THE HEART

POEMS OF SARA TEASDALE

EDITED AND INTRODUCED BY

WILLIAM DRAKE

MACMILLAN PUBLISHING COMPANY
NEW YORK
COLLIER MACMILLAN PUBLISHERS
LONDON

Library of Congress Cataloging in Publication Data

Teasdale, Sara, 1884-1933.
Mirror of the heart.

Includes index.
I. Drake, William.   II. Title.
PS3539.E15A6   1984   811'.52   84-7192
ISBN 0-02-616870-7

10   9   8   7   6   5   4   3   2   1

Printed in the United States of America

The following poems first appeared in POETRY: "Conflict,"
"Nights Without Sleep," "To a Loose Woman," "Afterwards,"
and "In Florence."

Contents

1914–1919

1920–1926

1927–1932

Introduction

by WILLIAM DRAKE

When Sara Teasdale made her will in May 1930, she directed that "no poems or verses of mine which remain unpublished at the time of my death shall be published after my death unless my written sanction for such publication appears thereon." She left all her papers in the hands of her friend and literary executor, Margaret Conklin. These included six small notebooks, about three inches by five, bound in red imitation leather, in which she had recorded and dated her poems over the years as she composed them. On the flyleaf of the last notebook she had written, "All poems that are not crossed out, can be published. S. T. December 30, 1931"; and added later, perhaps shortly before her suicide, "Name of the book to be 'Strange Victory.'" Margaret Conklin faithfully carried out her wishes, and the volume *Strange Victory*, consisting of twenty-two new poems, came out in November 1933, ten months after the poet's death.

Over fifty additional poems remained in the notebooks unpublished, many of them equal to her best work. The reason she withheld them, she had explained to Margaret Conklin, was that they were too revealing; friends might recognize references to themselves or to feelings and attitudes she preferred to keep hidden in privacy. Now, a half century after her death, and with the passing of virtually everyone who knew her, her fear of causing pain or embarrassment has lost its force. And the side of her personality that she wished to shield from public view has taken on more interest than the pleasant mask she assumed for her admirers. Consequently, Miss Conklin, with the sanction of the Morgan Guaranty Trust Company, legal executors of the Teasdale estate, has released Sara Teasdale's unpublished poems for inclusion in this new selection of her work on the occasion of the one-hundredth anniversary of her birth, August 8, 1884.

The unpublished poems, despite Sara Teasdale's fear of exposure, do not contain any startling revelations or new information. Whatever specific references they may have held have evaporated with time. Yet taken as a whole, they do reveal a more somber and troubled psyche than the tenor of her *Collected Poems* suggests. One is struck by the frequent allusions to a ceaselessly bleeding inner wound, to suppressed nervous anxiety, to feelings of worthlessness, entrapment, and despair. There is a surprising familiarity with thoughts of violence. This is the shadow side of a poet who strove to turn her painful and threatening inner experience into something calm and lovely, harmonious and acceptable.

In fact, Sara Teasdale believed that the source of her art lay in disturbances of the soul—"psychological" seems too reductive a term—and that the creation of a poem was an act of transforming destructive energy into something peaceful and beautiful. This is succinctly stated in an early poem, "Alchemy":

> I lift my heart as spring lifts up
> A yellow daisy to the rain;
> My heart will be a lovely cup
> Altho' it holds but pain.
>
> For I shall learn from flower and leaf
> That color every drop they hold,
> To change the lifeless wine of grief
> To living gold.

A marginal notation in her notebook, where she entered "Alchemy" on March 10, 1913, says "4:00 A.M."—a laconic indication that she had spent another night tossing in insomnia until this poem precipitated her torment into manageable form.

She formulated her experience into theory in 1919 for Marguerite Wilkinson's book *New Voices*:

My theory is that poems are written because of a state of emotional irritation. It may be present for some time before the poet is conscious of what is tormenting him. The emotional irritation springs, probably, from subconscious combinations of partly forgotten thoughts and feelings. Coming together, like electrical currents in a thunderstorm, they produce a poem . . . The poem is written to free the poet from an emotional burden. Any poem not so written is only a piece of craftsmanship.

This saving act of transformation had deep roots in her childhood. She once wrote to a friend that as a small child she used to put herself to sleep by telling stories to herself, "funny little tales" that would get her mind off her anxieties. An unfinished poem in her notebooks tells of lying in bed with "shivering fears" of the fitful sheet lightning while listening to an older boy across the street playing his mandolin on the lawn, as he became in her imagination a "minstrel knight" around whom she could spin stories. From the earliest time she could remember, the soothing music of language, the "solace of song," rescued her from threatening emotions that arose within herself. "As soon as a thing is nicely arranged in rhyme and meter," she wrote her friend Marion Cummings, "it ceases to bother one."

While the transforming function of art may be in some sense universal, for Sara Teasdale its origins and shape were peculiarly Victorian. She was the late, unplanned child of a well-to-do St. Louis wholesaler of dried fruits and nuts, with a long line of ministers and judges in his background. Her mother was the proud descendent of Simon Willard, a founder of Concord, Massachusetts, and her family line included a president of Harvard and a signer of the Declaration of Independence, as well as some notable clerics. The stiflingly proper atmosphere of Sara Teasdale's home, its prosperous middle-class gentility, its oppressive weight of Baptist morality and inhibitions, were among the things her generation of writers and artists were about to revolt against. Their rebellion was to be especially directed against the moral idealizing of this class, which in the glare of a modern realistic outlook seemed false and self-deluding. Freud and writers like Ibsen and Shaw were beginning to strip away the high-minded proprieties that overlay black depths of unacknowledged emotion. The task that presented itself to Teasdale's imagination, the consequence of being born when and where she was, was to deal with shameful, rebellious, or otherwise improper thoughts that were at odds with the requirement to be "nice," agreeable and ladylike at all times.

Isolated like a princess in a tower, as her St. Louis friends remembered her, Sara Teasdale was extravagantly sheltered by her aging parents, treated like a precious invalid and even kept from school until the age of nine. The result was a life of shy withdrawal and a tendency to be completely absorbed in herself. What seems to have weighed on her most heavily was an excruciating sense of invalidism, which she believed prevented her from participating in the normal physical activities of life. She guarded her energy by continual resting—the recommended cure in those days for the mysterious maladies of women—by escapes to country inns, even occasional stays in a sanitorium in Cromwell, Connecticut, and by wrapping herself against chronic colds and sore throats. She was periodically assailed by bizarre convictions about her body—she believed, for example, that she had been born lacking an outer layer of skin—or her health, claiming disingenuously that "my doctor" had told her of these things. Her nights were often an exhausting round of insomnia, for which she took Veronal from the early 1920s until her death from a drug overdose in 1933.

Stricken and sometimes incapacitated as she was, Sara Teasdale did not feel sorry for herself, nor did she lack creative vigor and courage. She sized up the enemy within and fought back. She possessed a first-rate mind, incisive and orderly, a keen business sense backed by ambition, and a shrewd ability to appraise people. In this dual nature—both receding and assertive, sensual and chaste, outwardly conventional and inwardly daring, frightened yet courageous—she resembled and was perhaps the last in the line of creative Victorian-era women like Christina Rossetti, Elizabeth Barrett, and Emily Dickinson. Her case differed from theirs, however, in that their strength through stoic self-denial, their triumphant resignation, no longer offered the terms on which a woman of intelligence could settle with life. A revolution was in the making. If Sara Teasdale had been fitted by background and breeding for the restricted, quiescent life of a Victorian lady, she was compelled to live that life, instead, amid the crash of war and social change and the release of women into the mainstream. "We cannot live through one of the crucial acts in the drama of civilization," she wrote, "without paying for the privilege."

As the gentle irony of this remark suggests, she felt somewhat ambivalent about that privilege. On the one hand, her childhood home and the settled values of her parents represented a cocoon of safety to which she was inordinately attached. On the other, she felt suffocated and imprisoned and longed to fly free as others were doing. At the age of twenty-six she still had to beg permission from her parents to travel to New York alone and was allowed to do so only after some of her more liberated St. Louis friends promised her mother they would look after her. She did finally achieve a measure of the hard-won independence, love, and success that modern women sought. But as many of her unpublished poems show, she could never wholly escape the crippling grasp of her upbringing, nor could she ever welcome the freedom of modern life without hesitation and misgiving. Her poems are virtually a record of her sometimes desperate inner negotiations, as "compromises wait / Behind each hardly opened gate."

In the early 1900s poetry was synonymous with "dreams," the ideal, rather than the real. The nineteenth century had ended on a hushed, transcendental note, with a worship of beauty as something far above and unrelated to sordid everyday life. Poetry was an appropriate field for a sheltered young lady to enter. This coincided with middle-class idealization of women, sexual purity, and sentimental Christianity. Male poets and ministers, because they supposedly dwelt on this level of uplift, were viewed as lacking in manhood and cut off, like women, from the life of action. It was the era that produced those delicate, effeminate Anglo-Saxonized portraits of Jesus, an artistic culture that modernist rebels would mutiny against with an outpouring of virile assertiveness.

Sara Teasdale intuitively seized upon the idealized image of women as of central importance and fascination. It defined what she, as a woman, was expected to live up to. The image of women had been explored in literature with increasing realism throughout the preceding century, although Teasdale's acquaintance with its range was fairly limited. She had been reared on the standard English classics in a private girls' school where the names of Balzac, Flaubert and Tolstoy, Hardy and Henry James, were unheard of. Yet she, like everyone else, was fully aware that the opposite side of the coin of the ideal was the "fallen" woman, the betrayer of sexual purity, sometimes ambivalently treated as a victim. With her instinctive attraction to the shadow side of experience, she turned for the heroines of her first poems to history's great fallen women whose tragedy and notoriety centered on their behaving with sexual freedom: Helen of Troy, Sappho, Guenevere. Her first poem to attract national attention and be widely reprinted was "Guenevere" (1907), a dramatic monologue inspired probably by one of Richard Hovey's proto-feminist verse dramas. Teasdale's Guenevere, guilty but proud, does not feel that in following the dictates of love she has done anything wrong, though she accepts her suffering as inevitable, a blending of the subversive with the submissive.

This glimmer of an awakening can be traced to Sara Teasdale's participation in an informal arts club called the Potters, formed by a group of young women in St. Louis in 1904 and continuing for about three years. They wrote, painted, acted, photographed, kept up with what was going on, and created a copy of a hand-lettered magazine once a month called *The Potter's Wheel*. They banded together, in effect, to prove that women could strive to attain a high level of professional competence and make names for themselves. Adolescent as the endeavor was, it was through this group that Teasdale learned to take seriously her talent and ambition, and to commit herself to the self-discipline, exacting self-criticism, and sense of craftsmanship necessary to sustain a career. It taught her that she had hidden strengths in spite of her family's effort to keep her virtually a dependent invalid, and made it impossible that she should ever bury her work in dresser drawers, like Emily Dickinson, or remain under the sheltering arms of brothers, fathers, or strong husbands like the women poets who preceded her.

High on the list of the Potters' idols was the great actress Eleonora Duse, who had performed in St. Louis. Actresses, by professional status, belonged to the category of fallen women, and Duse had furthermore suffered through a notorious and internationally publicized love affair with Gabriele D'Annunzio, which the young women romanticized heavily. Virtually throughout history such women who left the domestic circle to seek independence or prominence—or to go without male protection and control for almost any reason—were in danger of being treated as sexually promiscuous or advertising their availability, unless they could shield themselves with a forbidding and "unfeminine" hardness. Creative assertiveness therefore carried with it a considerable anxiety and risk to one's personal reputation. It was impossible to conceive of a dynamic woman without errant sexuality at the core of her being, victimizing her, like Guenevere, "whom Love so lashed, and with such cruel thongs." Such images, popular in Victorian culture, were a warning to women; and yet they contained a subversive element of defiance that Teasdale and her friends were quick to grasp. Duse's aloof and impassioned sadness embodied for the Potters the inevitable fate of women: if they expressed their nature freely, they would have to suffer for it.

Although she herself never saw Duse in person, Sara Teasdale wrote a set of sonnets to Duse, comparing her with Sappho and the Venus de Milo, her beautiful face "Carved in the silence by the hand of Pain." Teasdale's parents indulgingly put up the money for a private printing of her first volume, *Sonnets to Duse and Other Poems*, in 1907. She sent copies to prominent poets, and Arthur Symons in London wrote a favorable review. She was avid to see her words in print, and from then on she industriously pursued a professional career, beginning in the safe shelter of her home.

One short lyric—"The House of Dreams"—has been salvaged from *Sonnets to Duse* for reprinting in this collection, because it states so succinctly the course on which she had embarked. She tried to dwell, she wrote, in a house of dreams and memories (suggesting her childhood home)—but the "Wind of Truth" roared outside, pulling her out into the world. When she returned to that house, "The Wind of Truth had levelled it." This inconspicuous poem, in retrospect, prophesies the experience of her generation, who saw the illusory peace, the world of dreams and ideals they had grown up in, swept away abruptly by a war and the need to confront harshly exposed realities. The poem shows Teasdale's readiness to cut the ties with the past and live in her own time.

One has only to read the poetry of the 1890s to understand what, to a poet, was meant by a house of dreams. Yeats's small cabin in "The Lake Isle of Innisfree" is the prototype of that refuge of the imagination, a place of isolation, peace, soft sounds and twilight colors, suffused with nostalgia and a deep longing to escape from daily life that flowed "on the pavements grey." James Joyce at the age of twenty-two heaped ridicule on the escapist older poets, including Yeats, in a broadside he printed at his own expense:

> That they may dream their dreamy dreams
> I carry off their filthy streams
> For I can do those things for them
> Through which I lost my diadem.

Someone had to do the work of redeeming the rejected aspects of life, from which the dreamy poets and righteous middle-class citizens wanted to flee. To Joyce it was the "Holy Office" of the artist to perform a catharsis for both himself and these others, to be willing to fall, to lose his halo, in order to restore the lost wholeness of life.

Opening forbidden doors, however, was unthinkable for a

woman in Sara Teasdale's position, even though she too was forced to confront a confused, repressive morality that held prisoner her instinctive life. The revolt of modernism in the arts was, after all, largely a masculine affair, with women assigned to supporting roles, chiefly to nurture or provide pleasure for the now heroized canon of male writers and artists. Stephen Dedalus, Joyce's alter ego in *A Portrait of the Artist as a Young Man*, after his famous assertion of freedom, is attracted to a young woman whom he barely characterizes beyond her dual appeal as an "innocent" and a "temptress," the familiar stereotypes of male fantasy. The bohemian life and the adventure into new forms of expression offered women mainly the opportunity to be nursemaids to male genius, like Sylvia Beach or Harriet Monroe; or to be a mistress, something the rebellious males considered an obligatory evidence of their manhood and their own liberation. If a woman was burdened with troublesome emotion that required resolution through her art—as Joyce sought creative resolution through his—she had to look to some literary tradition of her own, to her predecessors who had defined the terms of femininity, rather than to men. Sara Teasdale, setting about the task of redeeming the inner pain of her life, had almost nothing to turn to but the conventional assumptions about themselves under which women poets had labored. And these women gave her examples of submission and suffering rather than rebellion—motherhood, marriage, losing themselves in men.

The young Sara Teasdale began by accepting the "truth" that a woman's life was created chiefly to love a man, even if it meant her unhappiness. Men had many other demands that came before love—work, achievement, adventure, creativity—but women did not. Teasdale actually knew very little about men from firsthand experience, so she lived in an imagination that was vivid from much practice. Through the years of her twenties she sat in her lonely study dreaming of the Great Passion that one day was supposed to sweep her off her feet, while writing poems of longing and disappointment.

Nearly half the poetic output of Sara Teasdale's lifetime was written before she was thirty. Her early popularity, her rise to prominence and the opportunities it gave her to meet other literary people as well as the man she was to marry, even eventually to escape from St. Louis and her family, all resulted from the open sesame of her poems. She had quickly realized that the Victorian poetic forms and rhetoric were dying, and that the future lay in simplicity and naturalness, the condensing of experience rather than the pretentious inflation of it. After a few early attempts at dramatic monologues and a verse play in Arthurian dress, she settled on the brief lyric as the appropriate form for her, and adhered to it with few exceptions throughout the rest of her life regardless of changing fashions. Of an ancient lineage going back to Sappho, whom Teasdale revered, the lyric bloomed periodically through the history of English literature. It offered a timeless frame in which the dance of the moment could be danced, a reassuring point of permanence in a tumultuous and dying world. The intensity of its statement was achieved through concentration and limitation, in language preferably limpid and unstrained, and with an air of effortless ease. Teasdale always called her poems "songs," in keeping with the traditional nature of the lyric as intended to be sung in accompaniment with musical instruments, originally a lyre. Many of her poems have, in fact, been set to music.

When Sara Teasdale discarded grand literary subjects in favor of personal emotion, her inexperience forced her into a narrow range. Yet what she had to offer was exactly what the public wanted. She did not calculate an image of herself; sincerity was an essential ingredient of her appeal. With the emergence of women into the work force and greater personal freedom as secretaries, teachers, and journalists, the public imagination had begun to shift from its prim Victorian perspective and head toward what eventually became the calendar girl, "America's sweetheart." When Sara Teasdale's poems first appeared in the years before World War I, they struck the perfect note for the time: an innocent eroticism yearning for experience, chastity straining toward sensuality. There is also a constantly reiterated complaint that being a woman denies one the freedom to take the initiative in love. This poem of 1911, for example, demurely titled "A Maiden," begins:

> Oh if I were the velvet rose
> Upon the red rose vine,
> I'd climb to touch his window
> And make his casements fine.

The rather startling suggestion of role reversal here, a woman climbing up to a man's window, is softened by stopping short at the windowsill to remain gracefully and passively ornamental. A further stanza says:

> But since I am a maiden
> I go with downcast eyes,
> And he will never hear the songs
> That he has turned to sighs.

The naive air of these early poems, coupled with a carefully restrained undertone of urgency and desire, suggests an impatience that is not prepared to wait forever. By continually hinting at what she is not allowed to say, the poet manages to get it across anyway.

This aggressive hunger for love and freedom of action had its dark side too: a rehearsal of expected death. Between Christina Rossetti's "When I am dead, my dearest" and Teasdale's "When I am dead and over me bright April / Shakes out her rain-drenched hair" lies an unbroken, morbid tradition that dwells on the inevitability of the death of beautiful women frustrated in love. Women often wrote as if from the grave. The poety of both Emily Brontë and Elizabeth Barrett acknowledged the link between loving and fatality, as if punishment is expected for taking the initiative. Emily Dickinson gave this feminine death-rehearsal an electrifying psychological immediacy. So it is not surprising that Sara Teasdale's quest for love and self-fulfillment has an air of laboring under a death sentence. The phenomenon is too complex for any capsule analysis, but one can see in Sara Teasdale's case a continuity between her suicide at the age of forty-eight and the lifelong counterimpulse toward self-negation whenever she ventured to assert herself in vital ways. Christina Rossetti and Emily Dickinson may have been made of sterner stuff in rising to virtuous resignation—both settled for the "white election," an austere, self-styled nunhood —but Teasdale could not accept that religious solution. She set up a little shrine to Aphrodite in her study and declared to a friend, "She is more real to me than the Virgin." Nevertheless, such a brave claim only set off an internal warfare between "Spartan and Sybarite," "Pagan and Puritan," which bedeviled her all her life and can be seen in particular intensity in the poems she did not want to publish.

Sara Teasdale's great opportunity to bolt from home came in January 1911, when she accepted an invitation to join the newly formed Poetry Society of America and traveled to New York for one of their first gatherings. She remained in New York for two months to make friends and establish a base of operations there among poets and editors. The burst of freedom is evident in a 1911 New York–inspired poem, "Union Square," in which she expresses envy of the prostitutes who can "ask for love," while she is forced by convention to keep silent. The poem appeared in her second volume, *Helen of Troy and Other Poems*, published by G. P. Putnam's Sons in the fall of 1911, and a startled reviewer in the *New York Times*, captioning his review "Woman Articulate," asked, "Has the woman who speaks in that very unusual poem, 'Union Square,' been always with us but inarticulate?" Teasdale had tried to say the same thing before but had concealed it in the chivalric, evasive imagery suitable for a lady writing about love, and so it had gone unnoticed. The notoriety of the poem made her uncomfortable, but she did forthrightly abandon the childish trappings of fairy-tale romance and cast her poems from then on in contemporary settings with increasing emotional honesty.

She returned to New York for lengthy stays whenever she could manage it, and in the summer of 1912 she toured Italy with a friend, the poet and reviewer Jessie Rittenhouse—a magical trip that culminated in a shipboard romance with a brilliant, erratic, and somewhat irresponsible young Englishman named

Stafford Hatfield, whom she compared to Shelley. It was her first taste of the Grand Experience she had been waiting for, but it ended in the shallows of confusion and disappointment. It is not clear whether he pressed her to marry him or just to go to bed, but in any case she dissolved in tears and "Like a coward I turned aside," as she confessed in an unpublished poem.

This failure compelled her to reassess her life more realistically. Approaching thirty, she concluded that she would have to get married soon or resign herself to being an "old maid." While the great romance could be foregone, marriage was a practical necessity to her, since she felt physically helpless to support herself and simply could not spend the rest of her life with her aging parents in a provincial city she now found unbearably dreary. In the space of a year she had learned to view romantic love with a measure of ironic detachment, so that when she met John Hall Wheelock and fell in love with him and his poetry, she worked very hard at inducing him to reciprocate. It was no longer a matter of the velvet rose climbing coyly to her lover's window to be admired: a woman simply had to take the situation in hand and, under the cloak of the conventions, get what she wanted while preserving her reputation.

However, although he was to remain a lifelong friend, Wheelock shied away from serious involvement. Matchmaking friends then stepped in. Harriet Monroe arranged for her to meet Vachel Lindsay, and Monroe's assistant, Eunice Tietjens, introduced Sara Teasdale to her own candidate, a St. Louis businessman named Ernst Filsinger. The spring and summer of 1914 were dedicated to setting poetry aside and grappling with the marriage question, with Lindsay and then Filsinger proposing to her, both of them pushed and encouraged from behind the scenes. She had not known either of them more than a few months and could not get her mind off Wheelock. Yet as if doomed to act out a ritual she did not have her heart in, she orchestrated a conventionally romantic courtship, giving consideration to one and then the other, stretching it out as long as she could stand up under the strain, in order to maintain self-respect before the world.

There was both comedy and pathos in this long-awaited event, and in the end, tragedy and unhappiness for all. Incapable as he was of supporting even himself, dominated by his mother and filled with visions about popular art that glorified the Midwest, antagonistic to the cosmopolitan culture of New York that Teasdale loved, Lindsay would have made a disastrous husband for her. Still, he was drawn to her for the critical intelligence and discipline he felt he lacked. What he really wanted, he confessed, was less a conventional wife than a companion to make him fulfill his own dreams, not an Eve to tempt him from his spiritual purposes. Doubtful of his course, he asked her to wait a year. Ernst Filsinger, on the other hand, was a reliable money-maker, a cultured, sensitive lover of poetry and the arts who appeared to have everything she wanted. Furthermore, he was desperately in love with her even before meeting her, through reading and memorizing her poems. She was, he wrote his parents, "my ideal for whom I have hoped since boyhood." With private misgivings, Teasdale accepted him as her only hope, telling Harriet Monroe, "I may be all wrong, but I can't help it." Their honeymoon in December 1914, she later told Wheelock, was a "fiasco." But she had gambled on what she believed she needed for survival: a man like her father, who could perpetuate the world of security and respectability she had depended on since childhood.

Real life began for Sara Teasdale with her marriage, in contrast to the feverish dream of perfect love that had preoccupied her for nearly a decade, for now the gap between conventional illusions and emotional actualities had to be faced. She wondered at first if marriage would silence her. Filsinger had written to his parents that she was a "glorious, *womanly* woman—no 'female rights' sort of person . . . Ever since I knew her she has put the duties of true womanhood (motherhood and wifehood) above *any* art and would I believe rather be the fond mother of a child than the author of the most glorious poem in the language." How much of this merely represents an impression he wanted to make on his parents and how much of it represents her actual assurances to him cannot be judged. But it is likely that she felt obligated to say something of the kind, since the marriage was in any case false to her deepest feelings. She had written to a male acquaintance in 1911, "A woman ought not to write. Somehow it is indelicate and unbecoming. She ought to imitate the female birds, who are silent—or if she sings no one ought to hear her music until she is dead." Dickinson comes to mind. "Art," Teasdale said, "can never mean to a woman what it does to a man. Love means that." Yet two weeks before her marriage, doubt surfaced enough for her to write the poem "I am not yours, not lost in you . . . I am I . . ."

Marriage, in fact, brought illness and depression. They had settled in St. Louis, from which she had hoped to escape, and after nearly nine months of continual, crippling bladder pain, and even more painful treatment, she had to be hospitalized. During this first year of marriage her husband, ever anxious to please, learned that this "no 'female rights' sort of person" was unyieldingly bent on going her own way. She insisted on separate bedrooms from the beginning, and she kept her own hours and made only half-hearted gestures toward domestic chores like cooking. In this period of adjustment Teasdale found herself no longer in love with love. She wrote to her young sister-in-law, "I used to always think that I wanted to lose myself in the man I loved. I see now that I can never do that, and that I was foolish to wish that I could. The man who wants a woman's brain, soul and body wants really only a slave. And the woman who wants to give *all* of herself, spirit and intellect and flesh, really doesn't want a lover but a master." These were "random thoughts that have come to me as a sort of shock since my marriage."

The change she was undergoing implied a profound change also in her work, an abandonment of the youthful themes on which her popularity had been based. But because of the lag between composition and publication, it was five years before her book *Flame and Shadow* disclosed the somber turn her imagination was taking. In the meantime she reaped the astonishing harvest of her early work and gained, to her lasting detriment, a reputation as a poet of adolescent moods, which overshadowed her more probing mature work. In 1915 the Macmillan Company published *Rivers to the Sea*, a collection of poems written mostly during the last few years before her marriage, reflecting her New York experience and her vain quest for Wheelock, who had provided the title of the book. *Rivers to the Sea* sold out in three months and went into additional printings. Pressed by her publisher for another collection to ride the wave of this success, she put together *Love Songs* in 1917, over half of it consisting of earlier poems in order to fill out the volume. *Love Songs* carried her popularity to new heights and won for her the first Columbia Prize for poetry in 1918, an adjunct to the Pulitzer awards. (The money was supplied by private donations, Pulitzer funds for poetry not being officially sanctioned until 1922.) Ernst Filsinger had found a job in New York in the midst of this outpouring of successes, bringing her at last to the glamorous city she had always wanted to live in.

Outwardly, it appeared that she had achieved all she had set her sights on only six years before, as a timid young woman venturing from the shelter of her parents' home. She was placed at the head table at the Poetry Society's annual dinners; her poems were read (though not by herself) before large groups at the New York Public Library and the National Arts Club; her name was familiar nationwide; she won additional prizes and probably earned more royalties in a year than many poets have done in their lifetimes. But already she had begun to turn her back on the Poetry Society, to find groups distasteful and fame a burdensome intrusion into her privacy.

It troubled her at first that the public might not care for the more austere and fatalistic moods of the poems she was now writing. Her life had seemed to reach its climax of fulfillment just as the war broke out, and the shock, the upheaval, and the aftermath of shattered ideals that pervaded the American people were reflected in herself. Not only the world that she knew, but her own life had crossed a divide. "Strange to have crossed the crest and not to know," she wrote in "The Long Hill" in 1919; "But it's no use now to think of turning back. / The rest of the way will be only going down." Her chief theme, the cry of unsatisfied love, continued after her marriage, changing, however, from a yearning for possible fulfillment to a mourning for what she had surrendered. She tried to accept the precept that since you can't have what you want, the best alternative is to stop wanting altogether: "Let it be forgotten." Or in another poem, "I have said goodbye to what I love; / With my own will I have vanquished my own heart."

Sara Teasdale was repeating the pattern of conflict and self-negation that had tormented her Victorian predecessors, but she lacked their spiritual resources for enduring it. Her own age was expansive, assertive, and grasping; stoic acceptance was the recourse of a loser. In a review-essay on H. G. Wells that she wrote for *The Little Review* in 1914, she had depicted her conflict as a debate between a modern woman and one whose conscience was still "a little old Victorian Lady." Poor Mary Martha goes about "imagining that I'm perfectly free." And then her conscience wakes up and says, " 'Stop that right now, I'm ashamed of you.' And she has authority, too, you know. I stop." Sara Teasdale always heard such an intimidating inner voice counseling her to be unassertive, obedient, humble, forbearing—traits that were considered to be feminine virtues, the inescapable "Mary" side of her nature. Rising against this voice was the unsettling power of the "Aphrodite" she had tried to follow on a road to freedom, love, and achievement. These two antagonists were too evenly matched for either to win a decisive victory.

John Hall Wheelock revealed in 1975 that Sara Teasdale had undergone an abortion early in her marriage, feeling that she could not continue her career and be a mother at the same time. Although corroborative evidence has not been found—her medical records, as well as her most intimate letters that might have referred to it, have been destroyed—there is no reason to doubt his word. A possible date can be assigned to August 1917, when she entered a poem in her notebook suggesting some emotional catastrophe:

> Fool, do not beat the air
> With miserable hands—
> The wrong is done, the seed is sown,
> The evil stands.

Shortly thereafter she admitted herself to the sanitorium at Cromwell, Connecticut, and through the following months sank into a state of physical weakness and severe emotional depression that lasted nearly a year. She never fully recovered. The need for frequent restorative rests in the country became habitual, and she complained of rapid exhaustion whenever she walked even short distances. This collapse into chronic emotional and physical illness was precipitated so suddenly as to suggest a specific catalytic event.

The war had also been deeply troubling. Teasdale and her husband, who had roots in the liberal German emigré culture of St. Louis, took an unpopular, though low-profile, pacifist position. She produced a number of poems contrasting the peacefulness of nature with man's insane frenzy to destroy himself. Her pacifism in response to the war projected on a cosmic scale the struggle within herself between peace and its violation, and her increasing need to find a safe refuge.

Although she had often turned when young to the Bible and the classics as a source of wisdom when deeply troubled, she had never felt any attraction toward the strict Christian faith of her forebears. While it had given them a toughness of character she envied, it seemed obsolete in present times. Her generation worshiped beauty and did not believe in giving things up. As her hope faded for personal fulfillment through love, she fashioned a salvation around the idea of the ecstatic experience of the beautiful. The problem was to find a way to compensate for suffering, to redeem it with something of equal value. In an unpublished poem, "In Sorrow" (1914), she had written,

> If out of the pain came pleasure, we might forgive it,
> But out of the pain comes nothing but pain again.

Life seemed to her a search for peace, balance, and harmony that, when attained, were soon shattered again. Two or three generations later she might have turned like many other Americans to meditation or yoga, for the experience of beauty as she presents it has the form of a spiritual encounter. She soon arrived at the idea of the brief, immeasurable moment as being equal to whatever amount of pain it might cost. An early formulation of this view appears in "Barter" (1916), where it is couched in terms of a financial transaction:

> Spend all you have for loveliness,
>   Buy it and never count the cost . . .
> And for a breath of ecstasy
> Give all you have been or could be.

A manuscript version of the poem has the alternate line "Life will not give but she will sell." The idea of an exchange, of a cost levied for the peak experiences that alone give life value, became a fixed aspect of her thinking.

Although this solution bore some resemblance to a spiritual, even mystical, pattern, it lacked the dimension of a transcendent reality in which the moment of individual ecstasy could participate in the divine mind and find permanence. Without this supporting center of her Platonic-Christian heritage, she found herself in an existential dilemma: what can be the value of even ecstatic personal experience when death wipes it all away? The moment of ecstasy therefore seemed like a very frail moment indeed, a mere flash in the blackness, like a shooting star.

At first she tried to salvage some hope of immortality from this precarious position ("The Wine," 1917):

> The rest may die—but is there not
>   Some shining strange escape for me
> Who sought in Beauty the bright wine
>   Of immortality?

This thought can be traced, as she felt its futility, to "The Wind in the Hemlock" (1918), where she tries to avoid the heroic loneliness of existential despair by lowering her consciousness to the level of nature, which, as beauty incarnate, is peaceful because it simply exists and asks no questions. Reading Saint Thérèse's *Vie d'une Ame* in 1920, she wrote to her husband, "The more one comes to think about life, the more one realizes it's necessary to get a certain amount of 'kick' out of it. But whether the 'kick' is obtained from sorrow, or joy, love, war, religion or art makes very little difference in the end."

In September 1919 Ernst Filsinger was sent on a lengthy business trip to South America and then, without a break, on to Europe in 1920 for six months more. Teasdale sublet their Manhattan apartment and moved to a hotel in Santa Barbara, California, for the time of his absence. She had begun to tire of the feverish, jazzy atmosphere of postwar New York, where an epidemic of broken marriages and sexual malaise only Freud could understand had broken out. In Santa Barbara she savored the hush of serenity and isolation in which the contending forces within her subsided for a while. She took up the study of astronomy, for the stars in their aloofness and orderly movements suggested a design in the universe to which one could give allegiance. If one had to bow one's proud head, it ought to be to something indisputably sublime. Submission of her will to another—whether to a man, a God, or a law of nature—was the one thing she had always felt she must do to attain the sense of being at peace with herself. In Santa Barbara she addressed the stars:

> With what unwearied patience you submit
> To the One Will that must be infinite—
> Your steadfast immortality
> Half angers and half comforts me.

She told Harriet Monroe that if she ever started a religion it would be star worship. The imagery of stars appears frequently in her work in the 1920s, but her finest lyric on the theme, and one with something of greatness in it, is one she never published —"In the Web" (1921)—in which the peace and dignity promised by the stars is no more than a sublime willingness to be trapped:

> Let be, my soul, fold your rebellious pinions,
>   There is no way out of the web of things,
> It is a snare that never will be broken,
>   And if you struggle you will break your wings.

[xxxvi]

Be still a while, content to brood on beauty;
    Caught in the trap of space that has no end,
    See how the stars, august in their submission,
    Take their Great Captor for their changeless friend.

The separation from her husband for nearly a year, in circumstances where she was almost constantly alone and absorbed in her own meditations, left her feeling detached and dreamlike. In subsequent years he traveled more and more frequently and she took her own time out alone, sometimes for weeks, in country inns around the Northeast. Their relationship, although settled and seemingly durable, had gradually come to seem less important to her than her own self-definition: "Let them think I love them more than I do," she wrote in "The Solitary" in 1921, "If it lifts their pride, what is it to me / Who am self-complete as a flower or stone." A process of withdrawal from Ernst Filsinger was under way, and one can perhaps see in it a pattern of attraction and aversion that originated with her Victorian father, the godlike figure whom she adored and wished to please, even though to do so made him, like God, not just her protective friend but her "Great Captor"; the definition of femininity as submissive, humble, ingratiating, has no reference except to male authority.

Sara Teasdale's father was, from all we know, a mild, kindly old gentleman, honorable in business and not a dictator or tyrant. He indulged her like a swan among ducklings, her friends said. When he died in 1921 she was immersed in grief and dreamed of him often at night for months afterward. Ernst Filsinger indulged her in much the same way, allowing her to arrange her life as she pleased and hastening to meet her needs the moment he was aware of them. In response to her spirit of self-determination, which must have threatened his idea of marriage, he may have sensed that a loving, overprotective provider could solidify a bond of dependence more surely than could an authoritarian will. The Victorians did not openly idealize the oppressor, after all, but rather the man who, through his generous and benevolent rule, received the voluntary homage from his subjects that he deserved. If Sara Teasdale had exited the stage of her childhood through her marriage, she found herself in the same cast of characters, playing out the same drama.

While Filsinger had been the prudent choice of a husband, Wheelock remained for her the dreamed-of lover with whom everything would have been different. Her poem "The India Wharf," written in the year after her marriage, commemorates a walk she took with Wheelock to the wharf, where they turned back. "I always felt we could have taken ship / And crossed the bright green seas / To dreaming cities set on sacred streams," a fulfillment of romantic love. Ironically, Wheelock was as unwaveringly in love with another woman, whom he married in later years, as Teasdale was with him and Filsinger was with her. Perhaps Wheelock's unavailability kept alive the fantasy. When her next book, *Flame and Shadow*, was published in 1920, it contained a dozen or more poems—including "Let It Be Forgotten"—written out of an attempt to reconcile herself to the hopeless persistence of this love. Characteristically, she held him close to her as a lifelong friend, and as a friend of her husband also, who could come and go in their apartment without any expression of her feelings that might compromise her marriage, a conflict held perfectly in suspense, "like stretched silver of a wave, / Not breaking, but about to break."

By the mid-1920s Sara Teasdale's productivity had begun to decline sharply as her feeling of being trapped in an inner struggle intensified and her outward life seemed more and more dreamlike. But as she wrote less, she wrote more skillfully. Her method had matured steadily not only through practice but through careful study of what other poets were doing, particularly Yeats, whom she considered the greatest poet of the time.

At the center of a lyric poem was always an implicit conflict whose tension played against its containment by rhyme and rhythm. For Teasdale the point of a lyric was not merely to state an emotion, certainly not to indulge in it or exploit it, but to clarify and analyze, to coax it from the dim regions of disquiet into consciousness. She wrote in *New Voices*:

Out of the fog of emotional restlessness from which a poem springs, the basic idea emerges sometimes slowly, sometimes in a flash. This idea is known at once to be the light toward which the poet is groping. He now walks round and round it, so to speak, looking at it from all sides, trying to see which aspect of it is most vivid. When he has hit upon what he believes is his peculiar angle of vision, the poem is fairly begun.

If the making of a poem was for her a process of attaining clarification and psychic equilibrium, this does not mean that the conflict at the heart of a lyric necessarily finds a solution. The result toward which the poem moves is more likely to be only a resting point, a moment of reconciliation that, despite its air of finality, contains the germ of a further disturbing question.

For example, the early poem "After Love" (1913) begins with the flat statement of the aftermath of a love affair: "There is no magic any more, / We meet as other people do." The second stanza develops the contrast by introducing imagery of the sea, the onetime greatness and "splendor" of the sea against the present reduction to a "listless . . . pool / Beside the shore." This defines being in love as a state of expansiveness, freedom, and power, as when a tide of greater life surges over an individual. But its withdrawal leaves a diminished sense of self, a separation from the greater whole. The third and final stanza swiftly unfolds from the sea imagery a complex and unexpected conclusion:

> But though the pool is safe from storm
> And from the tide has found surcease,
> It grows more bitter than the sea
> For all its peace.

The experience of love, it seems, is not only exhilarating but dangerous, so that along with its attraction comes a counterurge to escape back into peace and safety. The seawater has bitterness in it; love is not an unmixed pleasure. But neither is peace, with its freedom from risk, when it is filled with the bitter residue of regret and self-knowledge.

The underlying search for equilibrium seems to have been Sara Teasdale's guide in shaping a poem, as it was in her life. "The planning of the pattern of a poem is largely unconscious with me," she wrote to an unidentified Professor Lewis in 1922.

[xxxix]

This reference owes more to the lengthening shadow of Freud than to the romantic idea of inspiration. When asked by Eunice Tietjens if she had ever written poems "in dreams or in other subconscious states such as delirium," she replied, "I never wrote one . . . With me the conscious mind is on the job at the same time as a sort of governess to the child." The comparison is quite suggestive. The undisciplined energy and preverbal movements of the child are the realm of the subconscious, where she said the pattern of a poem was planned. "The patterns of most of my lyrics," she told Professor Lewis, "are a matter of balance and speed rather than a matter of design which can be perceived by the eye." She spoke of a rising and subsiding, a speeding up and slowing down, a balancing and echoing. The energies of the subconscious thus emerge as a set of harmonized contrasts rather than disturbing conflicts. The lyric moves by a kind of dialectic, and often the word "but" appears at a critical shifting point, with its implication of opposites at work against each other.

Sara Teasdale's characterization of her monitoring consciousness as a governess is somewhat chilling, for it reveals a certain primness in her dealings with the vital forces. And it throws light on the discomfort she felt in moving away from traditional verse forms and metrical conventions. She told an interviewer in 1922 that she had written her first verses at the age of fifteen, and "one of the bad rhymes, 'dusk' and 'trust,' haunts me to this day." Dissonances and spasmodic or irregular rhythms, which entered modern poetry along with the upsurge of hitherto censored contents of the personality, always repelled her. Her work is classical in its respect for form as harmonious containment, as a kind of established authority. Conventional form also offered a common meeting ground with the public, a fact of immense importance to women writers at a time when eccentric experimentation might have caused them to be laughed to discouragement and oblivion. Emily Dickinson has been honored for the bold dissonances of her poems, but they were achieved at the cost of almost total suppression during her lifetime, a trade-off not congenial to a woman aiming at public recognition and acceptance.

If Sara Teasdale was not in sympathy with forces of change that struck her as disintegrative rather than creative, she was nevertheless in tune with other progressive trends and made her own contribution to them. Before imagism she had seen the need to discard the Victorian clutter of generality and concentrate on the concreteness and immediacy of the image. Before Pound's dictum "to compose in the sequence of the musical phrase, not in the sequence of a metronome," she had seen the desirability of resisting the tyranny of over-careful counting or forcing of stresses and syllables, filling her verse patterns instead with the subtle irregularities of natural phrase-lengths and speech rhythms. If the following stanza is read in slow motion, its artistry emerges:

> I listened, there was not a sound to hear
>   In the great rain of moonlight pouring down,
> The eucalyptus trees were carved in silver,
>   And a light mist of silver lulled the town.

This is not as easy to write as it may seem: the pause after "listened" that creates a hush in which to listen, the heaviness of the two accented words "great rain" balanced against the lighter "light mist" in the last line, the unobtrusive repetition of "silver" that intensifies a key impression, the alliterative echoes of "carved" and "silver" and of the carefully spaced sibilants, the internal near-rhyme of "sound" and "down," the deliberate ambiguity of exactly how many primary stresses there are in three of the four lines, the absolutely conversational vocabulary, the coherence of the sentence as a whole whose slow movement and planned pauses define a great spaciousness while never diverging from the grammatical pattern of ordinary speech. By sparse use of metaphor she concentrates attention on one single memorable figure of speech, the "great rain of moonlight." But this has a purpose. The drenching noise of rain rendered soundless by its application to insubstantial moonlight evokes a silent world, a different consciousness emerging mystically from the heavier sensations of the ordinary stormy world, unrest transmuted to serenity. This may be a delicate, refined, and understated art, but it is art of exacting skill and a certain unique purity. Even Conrad Aiken, Teasdale's most hostile critic, conceded that she was "equipped with a very striking technical skill."

Sara Teasdale noticed the remarkable fact that from the middle of the nineteenth century poetry by women had flourished more abundantly than at almost any other time in history. In 1917 she edited the first twentieth-century anthology of poems in English by women, *The Answering Voice*, the title reflecting her view that poetry by women was a supplement to the dominant tradition of men and not in competition with it. "In most cases the finest utterance of women poets has been on love," she wrote in her preface, so her collection was limited to a hundred love lyrics, omitting any of her own. She arranged them in a sequence that traced the love experience from its awakening to its loss or death, beginning with Christina Rossetti's "Somewhere or Other" and ending with Emily Brontë's "Remembrance." The volume is a distillation of the feminine tradition in poetry before World War I, with an emphasis on idealistic, unsatisfied yearning, disappointment, and memories. In 1928 Teasdale reissued the collection with the addition of fifty new poems appearing during the decade since 1917. The landscape in that short time had altered radically. A new attitude "may be traced to the growing economic independence of women consequent on education," and the fact that women

have been forced to write because they found nothing to hand that expressed their thoughts . . . There is a wider range of feeling as well as a less conventional treatment in contemporary poetry. One finds little now of that ingratiating dependence upon the beloved, those vows of eternal and unwavering adoration . . . little, too, of the pathetic despair so often present in the earlier work. To-day there is stated over and over, perhaps at times overstated, the woman's fearlessness, her love of change, her almost cruelly analytical attitude . . . This is a period of transition. The perfect balance between the heart and the mind, the body and the spirit, is still to be attained.

She found that love was receding as the focus in women's poetry, and some fine poets, like Marianne Moore, had to be omitted from an anthology of love lyrics.

These two editions of *The Answering Voice* reflect a decade of profound change in Sara Teasdale herself. For by 1928 she had reached the decision to reverse her steady drift into emotional anesthesia by daring to act. "I could take the heavy wheel of the world and break it," she had written, "But we sit brooding while the ashes fall." In the summer of 1929 she fled secretly to Reno, having waited until Filsinger had sailed to South Africa on another long business trip, and sent him notice of her intention to obtain a divorce. Although reluctant and badly shaken, he was persuaded to comply. She returned to New York feeling that at last she was free to conduct her life as she pleased and concentrate on her writing as never before, in a place completely her own. Friends could not see what she had gained, since she had established a very independent life within her marriage and already did pretty much as she pleased. But it was an inner and not an outer tyrant that she was trying to unthrone. She was deeply pained by the irony of having to accuse her husband, for legal purposes, of having neglected her when it was she who wanted to be free of him. She had accumulated a cloud of frightening ghosts over the years of her marriage, and divorce was supposed to exorcise them. A smothered emotional violence erupted at intervals in imagery of death or madness, a "great black vulture circling the sky," a black hawk that "sweeps down and slays," a house afire, a sinister figure prowling in the night, a bloody fight to the death, the dripping of her own blood. At such times her own work seemed "useless as ashes."

But alone in New York—she refused to see Filsinger for two years—and withdrawn from most of her friends, she found herself more depressed than ever, her creativity virtually drying up; one of her few comforts was her friendship with the young Margaret Conklin, who reminded her of herself and became for her, she said, the child she had never had. After *Dark of the Moon* in 1926, she would publish only one other volume before her death, a small selection of her poems for children, *Stars To-Night*, in 1930. This she dedicated to Margaret Conklin.

The rebellion had come too late and only seemed to intensify her problems. In 1931 she tried to rouse herself by work on a critical biography of Christina Rossetti, about forty typed pages of which were completed before her death. Vachel Lindsay's suicide in December 1931 brought her to the edge of emotional collapse, perhaps because it shocked her with the reality of what had long lain in her own mind. She never recovered her balance. But in the last two anxiety-ridden years of her life she began to write lyrics again and produced some of her most perfectly achieved and moving work, as if the imminence of certain death gave her the sense of peace and assurance she had so long been looking for. She returned from a trip to England in September 1932 critically ill with pneumonia and hoping she might die. She recovered. But in the early morning hours of January 29, 1933, she drew a bath, swallowed the handful of sleeping pills she had been hoarding, and lay down in the warm water where her body was found a few hours later.

> Oh to let go, without a cry or call
> That can be heard by any above ground,

she had written in the sonnet "Wisdom" in 1931,

> It is all one, the coming or the going,
> If I have kept the last essential me.
> If that is safe, then I am safe indeed,
> It is my citadel, my church, my home,
> My mother and my child, my constant friend;
> It is my music . . .

Over the years she had survived by keeping opposing forces in balance rather than by choosing sides; for whichever won, "When the end has come, / I shall be the defeated one." She left her husband but tried to gain a child; pushed herself to define, in her own right, the "essential me" but gave herself to the waiting void. Her final transaction was paradoxical, a full payment that was yet another act of defiance.

Sara Teasdale's work occupies a unique place in the history of American poetry and the changing fortunes of women in modern life. Out of the large band of women publishing poetry before

[xliv]

World War I, she was the first to rise to a level of professional competence and national popularity comparable to that of men. And she did so not by couching her themes in male terms, or under the cover of religion, but by consciously writing as a woman of feminine experience. Her experience was that of a sensitive and often hesitant woman struggling to free herself from entrapment by the potent psychological forces that denied women fulfillment in terms other than wife, mother, or lover; a will to power confronting its own powerlessness. Her work was both her means of escape and her profound personal record, beginning as a conventional girl anxious to be loved, ending as a victim of her own attempted rebellion.

"And above everything remember your own fineness and be proud of it," she once advised her young sister-in-law. Near the end of her life she wrote in "Truce,"

> Pride, the lone pennon, ravelled by the storm-wind
> Stands in the sunset fires.

Feminine pride was her great discovery, the sustaining factor for a woman in any position of life or death. In this she had touched the deepest need of women in her time.

This new selection of Sara Teasdale's poetry is intended to offer a fresh and differently proportioned picture of her achievement in an entirely new arrangement. A large quantity of her immature work has been omitted, in order for her mature growth and lines of development to show more clearly. The poems have been placed in chronological order and dated, using the dates given in her notebooks. In a few cases where dates or manuscripts are missing, an approximation is given. Poems not titled by Teasdale herself have been indicated by brackets. The fifty-one previously unpublished poems have been inserted into their appropriate places in the chronology. In addition to these, fifteen uncollected poems have been gathered from magazines, and five have been sifted from out-of-print volumes, pieces that were not used in *The Collected Poems of Sara Teasdale*, which was first issued in 1937. The reader will find listed in an appendix to the volume all the newly gathered poems and their sources. The manuscript versions of two poems, "Song Making" and "Only in Sleep," have been used rather than the versions she published, because they differ in important ways. The previously published texts will be found in the appendix for comparison.

Acknowledgments

An incalculable debt is owing to the late Margaret C. Conklin, who first suggested and gave much valuable critical insight toward the preparation of this edition, in addition to her approval as Literary Executor of the Estate of Sara Teasdale. Brief excerpts from the letters and other writings of Sara Teasdale have also been quoted with the permission of Margaret C. Conklin.

Grateful acknowledgment is also given to the Beinecke Rare Book and Manuscript Library of Yale University for their permission to publish the poems of Sara Teasdale from the manuscript notebooks in their possession, with particular thanks to David Schoonover, Curator, Collection of American Literature.

I might have sung of the world
    And said what I heard them say
Of the vast and passing dream
    Of today and yesterday.

But I chose to tell of myself,
    For that was all I knew—
I have made a chart of a small sea,
    But the chart I made is true.

                    1919

1907-1913

1907-1913

THE HOUSE OF DREAMS

I built a little House of Dreams,
    And fenced it all about,
But still I heard the Wind of Truth
    That roared without.

I laid a fire of memories
    And sat before the glow,
But through the chinks and round the door
    The wind would blow.

I left the House, for all the night
    I heard the Wind of Truth;—
I followed where it seemed to lead
    Through all my youth.

But when I sought the House of Dreams,
    To creep within and die,
The wind of Truth had levelled it,
    And passed it by.

                  c. 1907

"I WOULD LIVE IN YOUR LOVE"

I would live in your love as the sea-grasses live in the sea,
Borne up by each wave as it passes, drawn down by each wave
    that recedes;
I would empty my soul of the dreams that have gathered
    in me,
I would beat with your heart as it beats, I would follow your
    soul as it leads.

                  c. 1910

[3]

THE KISS

I hoped that he would love me,
  And he has kissed my mouth,
But I am like a stricken bird
  That cannot reach the south.

For though I know he loves me,
  To-night my heart is sad;
His kiss was not so wonderful
  As all the dreams I had.

                    c. 1910

VOX CORPORIS

The beast to the beast is calling,
  And the mind bends down to wait;
Like the stealthy lord of the jungle,
  The man calls to his mate.

The beast to the beast is calling,
  They rush through the twilight sweet—
But the mind is a wary hunter;
  He will not let them meet.

                    c. 1910

YOUTH AND THE PILGRIM

Gray pilgrim, you have journeyed far,
  Swear on my sword to me,
Is there a land where Love is not,
  By shore of any sea?

For I am weary of the god,
  And I would flee from him
Though I must take a ship and go
  Beyond the ocean's rim.

"There is a place where Love is not,
But never a ship leaves land
Can carry you so quickly there
As the sharp sword in your hand."

c. 1910

THE SEA-GRAVE

We buried her out in the open sea,
Far from the lights and the harbor bars,
Deep in the waves where she longed to be,
Under a sky of stars.

The sea was tired and still that night,
It took her in forevermore.
Our boat that bore a crimson light
Turned back to find the shore.

And when we reached the restless quay
Our hearts were envious of her
Who lay too deep beneath the sea
For any storm to stir.

1911

I SHALL NOT CARE

When I am dead and over me bright April
Shakes out her rain-drenched hair,
Tho' you should lean above me broken-hearted,
I shall not care.

I shall have peace, as leafy trees are peaceful
When rain bends down the bough,
And I shall be more silent and cold-hearted
Than you are now.

1911

[5]

UNION SQUARE

With the man I love who loves me not,
　I walked in the street-lamps' flare;
We watched the world go home that night
　In a flood through Union Square.

I leaned to catch the words he said
　That were light as a snowflake falling;
Ah well that he never leaned to hear
　The words my heart was calling.

And on we walked and on we walked
　Past the fiery lights of the picture shows—
Where the girls with thirsty eyes go by
　On the errand each man knows.

And on we walked and on we walked,
　At the door at last we said good-bye;
I knew by his smile he had not heard
　My heart's unuttered cry.

With the man I love who loves me not
　I walked in the street-lamps' flare—
But oh, the girls who ask for love
　In the lights of Union Square.

1911

TO ONE AWAY

I heard a cry in the night,
　A thousand miles it came,
Sharp as a flash of light,
　My name, my name!

[6]

It was your voice I heard,
    You waked and loved me so—
I send you back this word,
    I know, I know!

1911

THE INN OF EARTH

I came to the crowded Inn of Earth,
    And called for a cup of wine,
But the Host went by with averted eye
    From a thirst as keen as mine.

Then I sat down with weariness
    And asked a bit of bread,
But the Host went by with averted eye
    And never a word he said.

While always from the outer night
    The waiting souls came in
With stifled cries of sharp surprise
    At all the light and din.

"Then give me a bed to sleep," I said,
    "For midnight comes apace"—
But the Host went by with averted eye
    And I never saw his face.

"Since there is neither food nor rest,
    I go where I fared before"—
But the Host went by with averted eye
    And barred the outer door.

1911

INDIAN SUMMER

Lyric night of the lingering Indian summer,
Shadowy fields that are scentless but full of singing,
Never a bird, but the passionless chant of insects,
  Ceaseless, insistent.

The grasshopper's horn, and far off, high in the maples
The wheel of a locust leisurely grinding the silence,
Under a moon waning and worn and broken,
  Tired with summer.

Let me remember you, voices of little insects,
Weeds in the moonlight, fields that are tangled with asters,
Let me remember you, soon will the winter be on us,
  Snow-hushed and heartless.

Over my soul murmur your mute benediction ·
While I gaze, oh fields that rest after harvest,
As those who part look long in the eyes they lean to,
  Lest they forget them.

1912

THE WAVE

I stood on the shore of the world,
 As one might stand by the sea,
And love, like a splendid wave
 Surged up the sand to me,

Terrible, full of song,
 Bearing its crown with pride,
But I feared the onward surge,
 Like a coward I turned aside.

Love, like a broken wave,
 Ebbed and the sand was bare,
Save where the flecks of foam
 Vanished into the air.

1912

[8]

THE RIVER

I came from the sunny valleys
    And sought for the open sea,
For I thought in its gray expanses
    My peace would come to me.

I came at last to the ocean
    And found it wild and black,
And I cried to the windless valleys,
    "Be kind and take me back!"

But the thirsty tide ran inland,
    And the salt waves drank of me,
And I who was fresh as the rainfall
    Am bitter as the sea.

1912

IMEROS

I am a wave that cannot reach the land,
    My strength is spent beneath a careless sky,
    Only the cruel sea-gulls, cold and high,
Glisten at last upon the restful sand.
I am a wave beneath the tempest's rod,
    Voicing the lost mid-ocean's shaken cry,
    I am a woman who will live and die
Without the one thing I have craved of God.
I am a harp with over-tightened strings,
    Where all the lonely winds of heaven come;
I am a singer, singing far and wide
    Who learns from longing all the songs she sings.
God, tho' my joy strike me blind and dumb,
    Send me not back to death unsatisfied.

1912

NIGHT SONG AT AMALFI

I asked the heaven of stars
    What I should give my love—
It answered me with silence,
    Silence above.

I asked the darkened sea
    Down where the fishers go—
It answered me with silence,
    Silence below.

Oh, I could give him weeping,
    Or I could give him song—
But how can I give silence
    My whole life long?

1912

.

OVER THE ROOFS

I said, "I have shut my heart
    As one shuts an open door,
That Love may starve therein
    And trouble me no more."

But over the roofs there came
    The wet new wind of May,
And a tune blew up from the curb
    Where the street-pianos play.

My room was white with the sun
    And Love cried out in me,
"I am strong, I will break your heart
    Unless you set me free."

1912

IN FLORENCE

I'm tired of all the quaintness
And the faded fresco's faintness,
Of dusty musty sacristies
With saints along the walls;
I'm very sick of Giotto
And Massaccio and Lotto,
And of dingy Lady chapels
With black worm-eaten stalls.

I'm sick of pictures by the mile
And virgins with an endless smile,
I'm tired of "things you ought to see"
And "things you ought to do."
I'd like to show these Florentines
What Broadway in Manhattan means,
And oh I'd like to walk today
Along Fifth Avenue!

1912

NIGHT IN ARIZONA

The moon is a charring ember
    Dying into the dark;
Off in the crouching mountains
    Coyotes bark.

The stars are heavy in heaven,
    Too great for the sky to hold—
What if they fell and shattered
    The earth with gold?

No lights are over the mesa,
    The wind is hard and wild,
I stand at the darkened window
    And cry like a child.

1913

ALCHEMY

I lift my heart as spring lifts up
   A yellow daisy to the rain;
My heart will be a lovely cup
   Altho' it holds but pain.

For I shall learn from flower and leaf
   That color every drop they hold,
To change the lifeless wine of grief
   To living gold.

1913

SPRING NIGHT

The park is filled with night and fog,
   The veils are drawn about the world,
The drowsy lights along the paths
   Are dim and pearled.

Gold and gleaming the empty streets,
   Gold and gleaming the misty lake,
The mirrored lights like sunken swords,
   Glimmer and shake.

Oh, is it not enough to be
Here with this beauty over me?
My throat should ache with praise, and I
Should kneel in joy beneath the sky.
O, beauty are you not enough?
Why am I crying after love,
With youth, a singing voice and eyes
To take earth's wonder with surprise?
Why have I put off my pride,
Why am I unsatisfied,—
I for whom the pensive night
Binds her cloudy hair with light,—
I, for whom all beauty burns

Like incense in a million urns?
O, beauty, are you not enough?
Why am I crying after love?

1913

DESERT POOLS

I love too much; I am a river
  Surging with spring that seeks the sea,
I am too generous a giver,
  Love will not stoop to drink of me.

His feet will turn to desert places
  Shadowless, reft of rain and dew,
Where stars stare down with sharpened faces
  From heavens pitilessly blue.

And there at midnight sick with faring,
  He will stoop down in his desire
To slake the thirst grown past all bearing
  In stagnant water keen as fire.

1913

SEA-SPRAY

You are the careless cliffs that shine,
  I am the wind and driven sea—
The ardor of the waves is mine
  And their futility.

Endlessly up the cliffs they yearn
  Breaking in song against the shore,
Silver sparks in the sun that burn
  And then go out forevermore.

1913

[13]

THE FOUNTAIN

All through the deep blue night
   The fountain sang alone;
It sang to the drowsy heart
   Of the satyr carved in stone.

The fountain sang and sang,
   But the satyr never stirred—
Only the great white moon
   In the empty heaven heard.

The fountain sang and sang
   While on the marble rim
The milk-white peacocks slept,
   And their dreams were strange and dim.

Bright dew was on the grass,
   And on the ilex, dew,
The dreamy milk-white birds
   Were all a-glisten, too.

The fountain sang and sang
   The things one cannot tell;
The dreaming peacocks stirred
   And the gleaming dew-drops fell.

1913

SWANS

Night is over the park, and a few brave stars
   Look on the lights that link it with chains of gold,
The lake bears up their reflection in broken bars
   That seem too heavy for tremulous water to hold.

We watch the swans that sleep in a shadowy place,
   And now and again one wakes and uplifts its head;
How still you are—your gaze is on my face—
   We watch the swans and never a word is said.

1913

AT NIGHT

We are apart; the city grows quiet between us,
    She hushes herself, for midnight makes heavy her eyes,
The tangle of traffic is ended, the cars are empty,
    Five streets divide us, and on them the moonlight lies.

Oh are you asleep, or lying awake, my lover?
    Open your dreams to my love and your heart to my words,
I send you my thoughts—the air between us is laden,
    My thoughts fly in at your window, a flock of wild birds.

                                                    1913

THE KISS

Before you kissed me only winds of heaven
    Had kissed me, and the tenderness of rain—
Now you have come, how can I care for kisses
    Like theirs again?

I sought the sea, she sent her winds to meet me,
    They surged about me singing of the south—
I turned my head away to keep still holy
    Your kiss upon my mouth.

And swift sweet rains of shining April weather
    Found not my lips where living kisses are;
I bowed my head lest they put out my glory
    As rain puts out a star.

I am my love's and he is mine forever,
    Sealed with a seal and safe forevermore—
Think you that I could let a beggar enter
    Where a king stood before?

                                                    1913

[15]

SWALLOW FLIGHT

I love my hour of wind and light,
  I love men's faces and their eyes,
I love my spirit's veering flight
  Like swallows under evening skies.
          1913

AFTER PARTING

Oh I have sown my love so wide
  That he will find it everywhere;
It will awake him in the night,
  It will enfold him in the air.

I set my shadow in his sight
  And I have winged it with desire,
That it may be a cloud by day
  And in the night a shaft of fire.
          1913

AFTER LOVE

There is no magic any more,
  We meet as other people do,
You work no miracle for me
  Nor I for you.

You were the wind and I the sea—
  There is no splendor any more,
I have grown listless as the pool
  Beside the shore.

But tho' the pool is safe from storm
  And from the tide has found surcease,
It grows more bitter than the sea,
  For all its peace.
          1913

THE STAR

A white star born in the evening glow
Looked to the round green world below,
And saw a pool in a wooded place
That held like a jewel her mirrored face.
She said to the pool: "Oh, wondrous deep,
I love you, I give you my light to keep.
Oh, more profound than the moving sea
That never has shown myself to me!
Oh, fathomless as the sky is far,
Hold forever your tremulous star!"

But out of the woods as night grew cool
A brown pig came to the little pool;
It grunted and splashed and waded in
And the deepest place but reached its chin.
The water gurgled with tender glee
And the mud churned up in it turbidly.

The star grew pale and hid her face
In a bit of floating cloud like lace.

1913

WRECKAGE

Love me less or more,
    Stay or let us part,
All that you can do
    Is to break my heart.

Sink my ship of love
    With its freight of gold,
Break it with black winds
    Where the sea is cold.

[17]

Still beneath the storms
    Miles and miles from shore
There is the buried gold
    On the ocean's floor.

1913

ON THE WIND

Joy goes by like a bird,
    Love goes by like a leaf,
But slow as an aged man's
    Are the steps of grief.

Catch joy if your wings can fly,
    And love if your feet can run;
But grief will still be there
    When the game is done.

1913

1914-1919

NIGHTFALL

We will never walk again
   As we used to walk at night,
Watching our shadows lengthen
   Under the gold street-light
   When the snow was new and white.

We will never walk again
   Slowly, we two,
In spring when the park is sweet
   With midnight and with dew,
   And the passers-by are few.

I sit and think of it all,
   And the blue June twilight dies,—
Down in the clanging square
   A street-piano cries
   And stars come out in the skies.

1914

DREAMS

I gave my life to another lover,
   I gave my love, and all, and all—
But over a dream the past will hover,
   Out of a dream the past will call.

I tear myself from sleep with a shiver
   But on my breast a kiss is hot,
And by my bed the ghostly giver
   Is waiting tho' I see him not.

1914

"I AM NOT YOURS"

I am not yours, not lost in you,
    Not lost, although I long to be
Lost as a candle lit at noon,
    Lost as a snowflake in the sea.

You love me, and I find you still
    A spirit beautiful and bright,
Yet I am I, who long to be
    Lost as a light is lost in light.

Oh plunge me deep in love—put out
    My senses, leave me deaf and blind,
Swept by the tempest of your love,
    A taper in a rushing wind.

1914

THE TREE OF SONG

I sang my songs for the rest,
    For you I am still;
The tree of my song is bare
    On its shining hill.

For you came like a lordly wind,
    And the leaves were whirled
Far as forgotten things
    Past the rim of the world.

The tree of my song stands bare
    Against the blue—
I gave my songs to the rest,
    Myself to you.

1914

[22]

THE ANSWER

When I go back to earth
And all my joyous body
Puts off the red and white
That once had been so proud,
If men should pass above
With false and feeble pity,
My dust will find a voice
To answer them aloud:

"Be still, I am content,
Take back your poor compassion,
Joy was a flame in me
Too steady to destroy;
Lithe as a bending reed
Loving the storm that sways her—
I found more joy in sorrow
Than you could find in joy."

1914

LEAVES

One by one, like leaves from a tree,
All my faiths have forsaken me;
But the stars above my head
Burn in white and delicate red,
And beneath my feet the earth
Brings the sturdy grass to birth.
I who was content to be
But a silken-singing tree,
But a rustle of delight
In the wistful heart of night—
I have lost the leaves that knew
Touch of rain and weight of dew.
Blinded by a leafy crown
I looked neither up nor down—
But the little leaves that die
Have left me room to see the sky;
Now for the first time I know
Stars above and earth below.

1914

THE WIND

A tall tree talking with the wind
    Leans as he leaned to me—
But oh the wind waits where she will,
    The wind is free.

I am a woman, I am weak,
    And custom leads me as one blind,
Only my songs go where they will
    Free as the wind.

1914

IN SORROW

It is not my own sorrow that opens my mouth;
Tonight it is the weeping of the world that shakes me.
I am lost for once in the ocean of men,
I am lost in a sea shoreless and black,
Wider than space,
Moving forever under a sky that is heavy.
In agony a child was born.
It was beautiful, but it died in an hour.
Yet the idiot with hanging hands cannot die.
He stands in the sun and frightens the passing children.
The old man shakes as he walks, and his eyes are pitiful,
They seek other eyes too feebly to draw their gaze.
They ask for comfort, they ask to forget the coming of death.
The young man dies in his youth.
His eyes had life to give and love to hold—
Where is his strength, who has taken it?
I heard the voice of the lonely thousands,
I heard them crying for joy before they die;
And the millions and millions of dead,
The undreamed-of millions—
What are we who have come from their sorrow and pain?
"It is spring," I said, "I will go to the fields for solace."
The orchard was bright with bloom, but against my face
The meek little petals kept falling, quietly falling.
Back to the earth they went with a frail reluctance.
A cat crept out through the fence by the shabby farm-house.
She caught a red-bird and bit through its feathery breast,
Bearing it off with a sneaking shyness
But never a touch of joy.

If out of the pain came pleasure, we might forgive it,
But out of the pain comes nothing but pain again.
What can I do
Where can I shed my blood
That those who are thirsty may drink?

[25]

Is my life a useless gift,
Even my life?

THE BROKEN FIELD

My soul is a dark ploughed field
   In the cold rain;
My soul is a broken field
   Ploughed by pain.

Where grass and bending flowers
   Were growing,
The field lies broken now
   For another sowing.

Great Sower when you tread
   My field again,
Scatter the furrows there
   With better grain.

1915

FLAMES

I watched a log in the fire-place burning,
   Wrapped in flame like a winding sheet,
Giving again with splendid largesse
   The sun's long gift of treasured heat.

Giving again in the fire's low music
   The sound of wind on an autumn night,
And the gold of many a summer sunrise
   Garnered and given out in light.

I watched a log in the fire-place burning—
   Oh if I too could only be
Sure to give back the love and laughter
   That life so freely gave to me.

1915

COME

Come, when the pale moon like a petal
    Floats in the pearly dusk of spring,
Come with arms outstretched to take me,
    Come with lips pursed up to cling.

Come, for life is a frail moth flying
    Caught in the web of the years that pass,
And soon we two, so warm and eager,
    Will be as the gray stones in the grass.

1915

SUMMER NIGHT, RIVERSIDE

In the wild soft summer darkness
How many and many a night we two together
Sat in the park and watched the Hudson
Wearing her lights like golden spangles
Glinting on black satin.
The rail along the curving pathway
Was low in a happy place to let us cross,
And down the hill a tree that dripped with bloom
Sheltered us,
While your kisses and the flowers,
Falling, falling,
Tangled my hair. . . .

The frail white stars moved slowly over the sky.

And now, far off
In the fragrant darkness
The tree is tremulous again with bloom
For June comes back.

To-night what girl
Dreamily before her mirror shakes from her hair
This year's blossoms, clinging in its coils?

1915

[27]

AFTERWARDS

I do not love you now,
  Nor do you love me,
Love like a splendid storm
  Swept us and passed.

Yet while the distance
  And days drift between us,
Little things linger
  To make me remember,

As the rain's fragrance
  Clings when the rain goes
To the wet under leaves
  Of the verbena,

As the clear rain-drops
  Cling to the cobwebs,
Leaving them lightly
  Threaded with stars.

1915

A PRAYER

When I am dying, let me know
That I loved the blowing snow
  Although it stung like whips;
That I loved all lovely things
And I tried to take their stings
  With gay unembittered lips;
That I loved with all my strength,
To my soul's full depth and length,
  Careless if my heart must break,
That I sang as children sing
Fitting tunes to everything,
  Loving life for its own sake.

1916

[28]

BARTER

Life has loveliness to sell,
  All beautiful and splendid things,
Blue waves whitened on a cliff,
  Soaring fire that sways and sings,
And children's faces looking up
Holding wonder like a cup.

Life has loveliness to sell,
  Music like a curve of gold,
Scent of pine trees in the rain,
  Eyes that love you, arms that hold,
And for your spirit's still delight,
Holy thoughts that star the night.

Spend all you have for loveliness,
  Buy it and never count the cost;
For one white singing hour of peace
  Count many a year of strife well lost,
And for a breath of ecstasy
Give all you have been, or could be.

1916

AUGUST MOONRISE

The sun was gone, and the moon was coming
Over the blue Connecticut hills;
The west was rosy, the east was flushed,
And over my head the swallows rushed
This way and that, with changeful wills.
I heard them twitter and watched them dart
Now together and now apart
Like dark petals blown from a tree;
The maples stamped against the west
Were black and stately and full of rest,
And the hazy orange moon grew up
And slowly changed to yellow gold
While the hills were darkened, fold on fold
To a deeper blue than a flower could hold.
Down the hill I went, and then
I forgot the ways of men,
For night-scents, heady, and damp and cool
Wakened ecstasy in me
On the brink of a shining pool.

O Beauty, out of many a cup
You have made me drunk and wild
Ever since I was a child,
But when have I been sure as now
That no bitterness can bend
And no sorrow wholly bow
One who loves you to the end?
And though I must give my breath
And my laughter all to death,
And my eyes through which joy came,
And my heart, a wavering flame;
If all must leave me and go back
Along a blind and fearful track
So that you can make anew,
Fusing with intenser fire,
Something nearer your desire;

If my soul must go alone
Through a cold infinity,
Or even if it vanish, too,
Beauty, I have worshipped you.

Let this single hour atone
For the theft of all of me.

1916

RICHES

I have no riches but my thoughts,
   Yet these are wealth enough for me;
My thoughts of you are golden coins
   Stamped in the mint of memory;

And I must spend them all in song,
   For thoughts, as well as gold, must be
Left on the hither side of death
   To gain their immortality.

1916

REFUGE

From my spirit's gray defeat,
From my pulse's flagging beat,
From my hopes that turned to sand
Sifting through my close-clenched hand,
From my own fault's slavery,
If I can sing, I still am free.

For with my singing I can make
A refuge for my spirit's sake,
A house of shining words, to be
My fragile immortality.

1916

IN A COPY OF *RIVERS TO THE SEA*
SENT TO THOS. S. JONES, JR.

Singer of many shining songs,
    Why do you ask for mine,
That have the scent of fallen leaves,
    Of winter-green and pine?

Go where the roses call you—
    Here only gray things are,
Unless through leafless branches
    You chance to see a star.

1916

IN ME

In me the quiet or the strife,
In me the dying or the life,
In me the lethargy or will,
In me the power to heal my ill,
And when my soul is parched with pain,
In my own heaven the fragrant rain.

1916

WOOD SONG

I heard a wood thrush in the dusk
    Twirl three notes and make a star—
My heart that walked with bitterness
    Came back from very far.

Three shining notes were all he had,
    And yet they made a starry call—
I caught life back against my breast
    And kissed it, scars and all.

1916

MASTERY

I would not have a god come in
To shield me suddenly from sin,
And set my house of life to rights;
Nor angels with bright burning wings
Ordering my earthly thoughts and things;
Rather my own frail guttering lights
Wind blown and nearly beaten out;
Rather the terror of the nights
And long, sick groping after doubt;
Rather be lost than let my soul
Slip vaguely from my own control—
Of my own spirit let me be
In sole though feeble mastery.

1916

WISDOM

When I have ceased to break my wings
Against the faultiness of things,
And learned that compromises wait
Behind each hardly opened gate,
When I can look Life in the eyes,
Grown calm and very coldly wise,
Life will have given me the Truth,
And taken in exchange—my youth.

c. 1916

[33]

SPIRIT'S HOUSE

From naked stones of agony
I will build a house for me;
As a mason all alone
I will raise it, stone by stone,
And every stone where I have bled
Will show a sign of dusky red.
I have not gone the way in vain,
For I have good of all my pain;
My spirit's quiet house will be
Built of naked stones I trod
On roads where I lost sight of God.

1916

AT MIDNIGHT

Now at last I have come to see what life is,
   Nothing is ever ended, everything only begun,
And the brave victories that seem so splendid
   Are never really won.

Even love that I built my spirit's house for,
   Comes like a brooding and a baffled guest,
And music and men's praise and even laughter
   Are not so good as rest.

1916

IN A BURYING GROUND

This is the spot where I will lie
   When life has had enough of me,
These are the grasses that will blow
   Above me like a living sea.

These gay old lilies will not shrink
   To draw their life from death of mine,
And I will give my body's fire
   To make blue flowers on this vine.

[34]

"O Soul," I said, "have you no tears?
    Was not the body dear to you?"
I heard my soul say carelessly,
    "The myrtle flowers will grow more blue."
                                            1916

SPRING RAIN

I thought I had forgotten,
    But it all came back again
To-night with the first spring thunder
    In a rush of rain.

I remembered a darkened doorway
    Where we stood while the storm swept by,
Thunder gripping the earth
    And lightning scrawled on the sky.

The passing motor buses swayed,
    For the street was a river of rain,
Lashed into little golden waves
    In the lamp light's stain.

With the wild spring rain and thunder
    My heart was wild and gay;
Your eyes said more to me that night
    Than your lips would ever say. . . .

I thought I had forgotten,
    But it all came back again
To-night with the first spring thunder
    In a rush of rain.
                                            1916

JEWELS

If I should see your eyes again,
　　I know how far their look would go—
Back to a morning in the park
　　With sapphire shadows on the snow.

Or back to oak trees in the spring
　　When you unloosed my hair and kissed
The head that lay against your knees
　　In the leaf shadow's amethyst.

And still another shining place
　　We would remember—how the dun
Wild mountain held us on its crest
　　One diamond morning white with sun.

But I will turn my eyes from you
　　As women turn to put away
The jewels they have worn at night
　　And cannot wear in sober day.

1916

WEARINESS

Oh let me be alone, far from eyes and faces,
　　Let me be alone, a while, even from you;
My soul is like a desert, sick of light-filled spaces,
　　The urge of useless winds, the sky of pitiless blue;
Let me be alone, a while, in twilit places,
　　Waiting the merciful night, the stately stars and the dew.

1916

[36]

SONG MAKING

My heart cries like a beaten child,
  Ceaselessly, all night long;
And I must take my own heart cries
  And thread them neatly into a song.

My heart cries like a beaten child,
  And I must listen, stark and terse,
Dry-eyed and critical, to see
  What I can turn into a verse.

This was a sob at the hour of three,
  And this when the first cock crew—
I wove them into a dainty song,
  But no one thought it true!
                            1916

SHIPS

One by one my dreams come true,
  Like tired ships into the harbor sailing,
With the tide at ebb and the watchers few
  And the low wind failing.

Yet one by one they creep to port
  Groping in when the fog is blind,—
One lost her cargo in a storm,
  Another was broken against the wind.

My wishes like slow ships return—
  But oh let love still rove the sea,
Bearing vague thoughts and old desires,
  Wandering and unfulfilled and free.
                            1916

[37]

SUNSET

(St. Louis)

Hushed in the smoky haze of summer sunset,
When I came home again from far-off places,
How many times I saw my western city
    Dream by her river.

Then for an hour the water wore a mantle
Of tawny gold and mauve and misted turquoise
Under the tall and darkened arches bearing
    Gray, high-flung bridges.

Against the sunset, water-towers and steeples
Flickered with fire up the slope to westward,
And old warehouses poured their purple shadows
    Across the levee.

High over them the black train swept with thunder,
Cleaving the city, leaving far beneath it
Wharf-boats moored beside the old side-wheelers
    Resting in twilight.

1917

RED MAPLES

In the last year I have learned
How few men are worth my trust;
I have seen the friend I loved
Struck by death into the dust,
And fears I never knew before
Have knocked and knocked upon my door—
"I shall hope little and ask for less,"
I said, "There is no happiness."

I have grown wise at last—but how
Can I hide the gleam on the willow-bough,
Or keep the fragrance out of the rain
Now that April is here again?
When maples stand in a haze of fire
What can I say to the old desire,
What shall I do with the joy in me
That is born out of agony?

1917

THE WINE

I cannot die, who drank delight
    From the cup of the crescent moon,
And hungrily as men eat bread,
    Loved the scented nights of June.

The rest may die—but is there not
    Some shining strange escape for me
Who sought in Beauty the bright wine
    Of immortality?

1917

DEBTOR

So long as my spirit still
    Is glad of breath
And lifts its plumes of pride
    In the dark face of death;
While I am curious still
    Of love and fame,
Keeping my heart too high
    For the years to tame,
How can I quarrel with fate
    Since I can see
I am a debtor to life,
    Not life to me?

1917

[39]

SPRAY

I knew you thought of me all night,
   I knew, though you were far away;
     I felt your love blow over me
     As if a dark wind-riven sea
   Drenched me with quivering spray.

There are so many ways to love
   And each way has its own delight—
     Then be content to come to me
     Only as spray the beating sea
   Drives inland through the night.

                 1917

THE LAMP

If I can bear your love like a lamp before me,
When I go down the long steep Road of Darkness,
I shall not fear the everlasting shadows,
     Nor cry in terror.

If I can find out God, then I shall find Him,
If none can find Him, then I shall sleep soundly,
Knowing how well on earth your love sufficed me,
     A lamp in darkness.

                 1917

BECAUSE

Oh, because you never tried
To bow my will or break my pride,
And nothing of the cave-man made
You want to keep me half afraid,
Nor ever with a conquering air
You thought to draw me unaware—
Take me, for I love you more
Than I ever loved before.

And since the body's maidenhood
Alone were neither rare nor good
Unless with it I gave to you
A spirit still untrammeled, too,
Take my dreams and take my mind
That were masterless as wind;
And "Master!" I shall say to you
Since you never asked me to.

1917

DOUBT

My soul lives in my body's house,
    And you have both the house and her—
But sometimes she is less your own
    Than a wild, gay adventurer;
A restless and an eager wraith,
    How can I tell what she will do—
Oh, I am sure of my body's faith,
    But what if my soul broke faith with you?

1917

DUTY

Fool, do not beat the air
    With miserable hands—
The wrong is done, the seed is sown,
    The evil stands.

Your duty is to draw
    Out of the web of wrong,
Out of ill-woven deeds,
    A thread of song.

1917

THE GAME

My heart is crying without sound
As blood wells up in an open wound;
"Life is a game," I said, "that I
Will play with laughter and head held high.
I will keep the ancient rules that none
Can laugh at me when the game is done;
I will play for love and a little fame—"
I played and I have won the game.
I have the things that I desired,
I am alone and very tired;
My heart is crying without sound
As blood wells up in an open wound.

1917

ALONE

I am alone, in spite of love,
    In spite of all I take and give—
In spite of all your tenderness,
    Sometimes I am not glad to live.

I am alone, as though I stood
    On the highest peak of the tired gray world,
About me only swirling snow,
    Above me endless space unfurled;

With earth hidden and heaven hidden,
    And only my own spirit's pride
To keep me from the peace of those
    Who are not lonely, having died.

1918

CHANGE

Remember me as I was then;
　Turn from me now, but always see
The laughing shadowy girl who stood
　At midnight by the flowering tree,
With eyes that love had made as bright
As the trembling stars of the summer night.

Turn from me now, but always hear
　The muted laughter in the dew
Of that one year of youth we had,
　The only youth we ever knew—
Turn from me now, or you will see
What other years have done to me.

1918

"ONLY IN SLEEP"

Only in sleep I see their faces,
　Children I played with when I was a child,
Louise comes back with her brown hair braided,
　Annie with ringlets warm and wild.

Only in sleep Time cannot hurt us—
　What may have come to them, who can know?
They are women now if they are living,
　Yet we played last night as long ago,
　With stealthy secrets whispered low.

Smooth round faces years had not sharpened,
　I met their eyes and found them mild—
Do they too dream of me, I wonder,
　I, an eager shadowy child
　Care had not darkened nor pain defiled?

1918

[43]

AT SEA

In the pull of the wind I stand, lonely,
   On the deck of a ship, rising, falling,
Wild night around me, wild water under me,
   Whipped by the storm, screaming and calling.

Earth is hostile and the sea hostile,
   Why do I look for a place to rest?
I must fight always and die fighting
   With fear an unhealing wound in my breast.

1918

IN A CUBAN GARDEN

Hibiscus flowers are cups of fire,
   (Love me, my lover, life will not stay)
The bright poinsettia shakes in the wind,
   A scarlet leaf is blowing away.

A lizard lifts his head and listens—
   Kiss me before the noon goes by,
Here in the shade of the ceiba hide me
   From the great black vulture circling the sky.

1918

THE NIGHTS REMEMBER

The days remember and the nights remember
   The kingly hours that once you made so great,
Deep in my heart they lie, hidden in their splendor,
   Buried like sovereigns in their robes of state.

Let them not wake again, better to lie there,
   Wrapped in memories, jewelled and arrayed—
Many a ghostly king has waked from death-sleep
   And found his crown stolen and his throne decayed.

1918

[44]

"MY HEART IS HEAVY"

My heart is heavy with many a song
    Like ripe fruit bearing down the tree,
But I can never give you one—
    My songs do not belong to me.

Yet in the evening, in the dusk
    When moths go to and fro,
In the gray hour if the fruit has fallen,
    Take it, no one will know.

                              c. 1918

THE COIN

Into my heart's treasury
    I slipped a coin
That time cannot take
    Nor a thief purloin,—
Oh, better than the minting
    Of a gold-crowned king
Is the safe-kept memory
    Of a lovely thing.

                              1918

THOUGHTS

When I am all alone
    Envy me most,
Then my thoughts flutter round me
    In a glimmering host;

Some dressed in silver,
    Some dressed in white,
Each like a taper
    Blossoming light;

[45]

Most of them merry,
  Some of them grave,
Each of them lithe
  As willows that wave;

Some bearing violets,
  Some bearing bay,
One with a burning rose
  Hidden away—

When I am all alone
  Envy me then,
For I have better friends
  Than women and men.

                          1918

OLD TUNES

As the waves of perfume, heliotrope, rose,
Float in the garden when no wind blows,
Come to us, go from us, whence no one knows;

So the old tunes float in my mind,
And go from me leaving no trace behind,
Like fragrance borne on the hush of the wind.

But in the instant the airs remain
I know the laughter and the pain
Of times that will not come again.

I try to catch at many a tune
Like petals of light fallen from the moon,
Broken and bright on a dark lagoon.

But they float away—for who can hold
Youth, or perfume or the moon's gold?

                          1918

[46]

PLACES

Places I love come back to me like music,
  Hush me and heal me when I am very tired;
I see the oak woods at Saxton's flaming
  In a flare of crimson by the frost newly fired;
And I am thirsty for the spring in the valley
  As for a kiss ungiven and long desired.

I know a bright world of snowy hills at Boonton,
  A blue and white dazzling light on everything one sees,
The ice-covered branches of the hemlocks sparkle
  Bending low and tinkling in the sharp thin breeze,
And iridescent crystals fall and crackle on the snow-crust
  With the winter sun drawing cold blue shadows from the
    trees.

Violet now, in veil on veil of evening,
  The hills across from Cromwell grow dreamy and far;
A wood-thrush is singing soft as a viol
  In the heart of the hollow where the dark pools are;
The primrose has opened her pale yellow flowers
  And heaven is lighting star after star.

Places I love come back to me like music—
  Mid-ocean, midnight, the waves buzz drowsily;
In the ship's deep churning the eerie phosphorescence
  Is like the souls of people who were drowned at sea,
And I can hear a man's voice, speaking, hushed, insistent,
  At midnight, in mid-ocean, hour on hour to me.

1918

DRIFTWOOD

My forefathers gave me
  My spirit's shaken flame,
The shape of hands, the beat of heart,
  The letters of my name.

But it was my lovers,
  And not my sleeping sires,
Who gave the flame its changeful
  And iridescent fires;

As the driftwood burning
  Learned its jewelled blaze
From the sea's blue splendor
  Of colored nights and days.   *1918*

BLUE SQUILLS

How many million Aprils came
  Before I ever knew
How white a cherry bough could be,
  A bed of squills, how blue!

And many a dancing April
  When life is done with me,
Will lift the blue flame of the flower
  And the white flame of the tree.

Oh burn me with your beauty, then,
  Oh hurt me, tree and flower,
Lest in the end death try to take
  Even this glistening hour.

O shaken flowers, O shimmering trees,
  O sunlit white and blue,
Wound me, that I, through endless sleep,
  May bear the scar of you.   *1918*

[48]

THE WIND IN THE HEMLOCK

Steely stars and moon of brass,
How mockingly you watch me pass!
You know as well as I how soon
I shall be blind to stars and moon,
Deaf to the wind in the hemlock tree,
Dumb when the brown earth weighs on me.

With envious dark rage I bear,
Stars, your cold complacent stare;
Heart-broken in my hate look up,
Moon, at your clear immortal cup,
Changing to gold from dusky red—
Age after age when I am dead
To be filled up with light, and then
Emptied, to be refilled again.
What has man done that only he
Is slave to death—so brutally
Beaten back into the earth
Impatient for him since his birth?

Oh let me shut my eyes, close out
The sight of stars and earth and be
Sheltered a minute by this tree.
Hemlock, through your fragrant boughs
There moves no anger and no doubt,
No envy of immortal things.
The night-wind murmurs of the sea
With veiled music ceaselessly,
That to my shaken spirit sings.
From their frail nest the robins rouse,
In your pungent darkness stirred,
Twittering a low drowsy word—
And me you shelter, even me.
In your quietness you house
The wind, the woman and the bird.
You speak to me and I have heard:

[49]

If I am peaceful, I shall see
Beauty's face continually;
Feeding on her wine and bread
I shall be wholly comforted,
For she can make one day for me
Rich as my lost eternity.

1918

THE STRONG HOUSE

Our love is like a strong house
  Well roofed against the wind and rain—
Who passes darkly in the sun
  Again and again?

The doors are fast, the lamps are lit,
  We sit together talking low—
Who is it in the ghostly dusk
  Goes to and fro?

Surely ours is a strong house,
  I will not trouble any more—
But who comes stealing at midnight
  To try the locked door?

1918

STRANGE

Strange that we two, who love all quiet things,
  Coves by the sea, with waves too small for foam,
Stars seen in water, love too sure for speech,
  And eyes that make for other eyes a home;

Strange that we two should choose this harried hour
  To leave whatever world we knew before
For this sick planet, with its tired hordes
  Locked in the grim fatality of war.

1918

[50]

"IT WILL NOT CHANGE"

It will not change now
    After so many years;
Life has not broken it
    With parting or tears;
Death will not alter it,
    It will live on
In all my songs for you
    When I am gone.

1919

TO E. IN SWITZERLAND

I like to think of you among still mountains
    Wearing bright immemorial capes of snow,
In their unbroken ancient meditation
    Far above noise and struggle of things that grow.

I like to think at last your hurried spirit
    Has found a cold white hour of calm to see,
As though you looked into a polished crystal,
    Life, its vast trifles and yourself and me.

1919

SLEEPLESS

If I could have your arms tonight—
    But half the world and the broken sea
    Lie between you and me.

The autumn rain reverberates in the courtyard,
Beating all night against the barren stone,
The sound of useless rain in the desolate courtyard
Makes me more alone.

If you were here, if you were only here—
    My blood cries out to you all night in vain
    As sleepless as the rain.

1919

[51]

[MY LIPS HAVE NOT COMPLAINED]

My lips have not complained,
    They have not said a word—
It must have been my stillness,
    If anything, you heard.
When you are far away
    And half the world around,
Silence travels
    Faster than sound.

1919

THE MYSTERY

Your eyes drink of me,
    Love makes them shine,
Your eyes that lean
    So close to mine.

We have long been lovers,
    We know the range
Of each other's moods
    And how they change;

But when we look
    At each other so
Then we feel
    How little we know;

The spirit eludes us,
    Timid and free—
Can I ever know you
    Or you know me?

1919

NIGHT AFTER NIGHT

Night after night under my window
To and fro paces a shadow;

Is it a man or a ghost I see?
Is it a lover wanting me?

I draw the curtain with caught breath
—I make no sign, I am free of blame,

Oh is it Love or is it Death,
Are they the same?

1919

WRAITHS

Up the wide wind-swept avenue
    A girl and her lover walk tonight—
They are not real, they are wraiths,
    They cast no shadow in the light.

A stinging winter wind is out,
    They are too happy to be cold,
The street lamps make a path for them
    And pave the empty street with gold.

Lightly they tread to an unheard flute,
    They are too happy to be talking—
Hush, they are wraiths, they are not real,
    Two gay young ghosts have gone out walking.

Into a doorway arched and dim
    He draws her, and the darkness there
Knows if she quivers to a kiss
    On lips and eyes and wind-blown hair.

Now they are fading, they are gone!
    Often on nights like these I see
The slight, triumphant, wilful thing,
    A wraith, the girl I used to be.

1919

[53]

SNOWFALL

"She can't be unhappy," you said,
   "The smiles are like stars in her eyes,
And her laugh is thistledown
   Around her low replies."
"Is she unhappy?" you said—
   But who has ever known
Another's heartbreak—
   All he can know is his own;
And she seems hushed to me,
   As hushed as though
Her heart were a hunter's fire
   Smothered in snow.

1919

THE TREE

Oh to be free of myself,
   With nothing left to remember,
To have my heart as bare
   As a tree in December;

Resting, as a tree rests
   After its leaves are gone,
Waiting no more for a rain at night
   Nor for the red at dawn;

But still, oh so still
   While the winds come and go,
With no more fear of the hard frost
   Or the bright burden of snow;

And heedless, heedless
   If anyone pass and see
On the white page of the sky
   Its thin black tracery.

c. 1919

[54]

DUST

When I went to look at what had long been hidden,
  A jewel laid long ago in a secret place,
I trembled, for I thought to see its dark deep fire—
  But only a pinch of dust blew up in my face.

I almost gave my life long ago for a thing
  That has gone to dust now, stinging my eyes—
It is strange how often a heart must be broken
  Before the years can make it wise.

1919

BELLS

At six o'clock of an autumn dusk
  With the sky in the west a rusty red,
The bells of the mission down in the valley
  Cry out that the day is dead.

The first star pricks as sharp as steel—
  Why am I suddenly so cold?
Three bells, each with a separate sound
  Clang in the valley, wearily tolled.

Bells in Venice, bells at sea,
  Bells in the valley heavy and slow—
There is no place over the crowded world
  Where I can forget that the days go.

1919

"OH DAY OF FIRE AND SUN"

Oh day of fire and sun,
  Pure as a naked flame,
Blue sea, blue sky and dun
  Sands where he spoke my name;

Laughter and hearts so high
  That the spirit flew off free,
Lifting into the sky
  Diving into the sea;

Oh day of fire and sun
  Like a crystal burning,
Slow days go one by one,
  But you have no returning.

1919

THE GARDEN

My heart is a garden tired with autumn,
  Heaped with bending asters and dahlias heavy and dark,
In the hazy sunshine, the garden remembers April,
  The drench of rains and a snow-drop quick and clear as a
    spark;

Daffodils blowing in the cold wind of morning,
  And golden tulips, goblets holding the rain—
The garden will be hushed with snow, forgotten soon, for-
    gotten—
  After the stillness, will spring come again?

1919

MAY DAY

A delicate fabric of bird song
 Floats in the air,
The smell of wet wild earth
 Is everywhere.

Red small leaves of the maple
 Are clenched like a hand,
Like girls at their first communion
 The pear trees stand.

Oh I must pass nothing by
 Without loving it much,
The raindrop try with my lips,
 The grass with my touch;

For how can I be sure
 I shall see again
The world on the first of May
 Shining after the rain?

1919

REDBIRDS

Redbirds, redbirds,
 Long and long ago,
What a honey-call you had
 In hills I used to know;

Redbud, buckberry,
 Wild plum-tree
And proud river sweeping
 Southward to the sea,

Brown and gold in the sun
 Sparkling far below,
Trailing stately round her bluffs
 Where the poplars grow—

[57]

Redbirds, redbirds,
    Are you singing still
As you sang one May day
    On Saxton's Hill?

1919

"IT IS NOT A WORD"

It is not a word spoken,
    Few words are said;
Nor even a look of the eyes
    Nor a bend of the head,
But only a hush of the heart
    That has too much to keep,
Only memories waking
    That sleep so light a sleep.

1919

IN THE END

All that could never be said,
    All that could never be done,
Wait for us at last
    Somewhere back of the sun;

All the heart broke to forego
    Shall be ours without pain,
We shall take them as lightly as girls
    Pluck flowers after rain.

And when they are ours in the end
    Perhaps after all
The skies will not open for us
    Nor heaven be there at our call.

1919

NOVEMBER STARS

Splendor of many stars and the unknown
Invisible lights with which all space is strewn,
With what unwearied patience you submit
To the One Will that must be infinite—
Your steadfast immortality
Half angers and half comforts me;
Serenely ordered, on and on
You will shine—I shall be gone.

1919

SPRING SONG

I went up the avenue
    In the April shine,
Many and many a man passed,
    But not one was mine.

I turned to pray in a church
    And from the tall choir
Men's voices were ringing
    Clear as fire.

"Let me go home," I said,
    "There, all alone
I will read a dull book
    As still as a stone;

"Home is the place for me
    On an April day—
There I can lock the door
    And keep spring away."

1919

[59]

MORNING SONG

A diamond of a morning
  Waked me an hour too soon;
Dawn had taken in the stars
  And left the faint white moon.

O white moon, you are lonely,
  It is the same with me,
But we have the world to roam over,
  Only the lonely are free.

1919

LOVELY CHANCE

O lovely chance, what can I do
To give my gratefulness to you?
You rise between myself and me
With a wise persistency;
I would have broken body and soul,
But by your grace, still I am whole.
Many a thing you did to save me,
Many a holy gift you gave me,
Music and friends and happy love
More than my dearest dreaming of;
And now in this wide twilight hour
With earth and heaven a dark, blue flower,
In a humble mood I bless
Your wisdom—and your waywardness.
You brought me even here, where I
Live on a hill against the sky
And look on mountains and the sea
And a thin white moon in the pepper tree.

1919

ON THE DUNES

If there is any life when death is over,
    These tawny beaches will know much of me,
I shall come back, as constant and as changeful
    As the unchanging, many-colored sea.

If life was small, if it has made me scornful,
    Forgive me; I shall straighten like a flame
In the great calm of death, and if you want me
    Stand on the sea-ward dunes and call my name.

1919

"I THOUGHT OF YOU"

I thought of you and how you love this beauty,
    And walking up the long beach all alone
I heard the waves breaking in measured thunder
    As you and I once heard their monotone.

Around me were the echoing dunes, beyond me
    The cold and sparkling silver of the sea—
We two will pass through death and ages lengthen
    Before you hear that sound again with me.

1919

IF DEATH IS KIND

Perhaps if Death is kind, and there can be returning,
    We will come back to earth some fragrant night,
And take these lanes to find the sea, and bending
    Breathe the same honeysuckle, low and white.

We will come down at night to these resounding beaches
    And the long gentle thunder of the sea,
Here for a single hour in the wide starlight
    We shall be happy, for the dead are free.

1919

[61]

"LET IT BE FORGOTTEN"

Let it be forgotten, as a flower is forgotten,
   Forgotten as a fire that once was singing gold,
Let it be forgotten for ever and ever,
   Time is a kind friend, he will make us old.

If anyone asks, say it was forgotten
   Long and long ago,
As a flower, as a fire, as a hushed footfall
   In a long forgotten snow.

1919

THE SANCTUARY

If I could keep my innermost Me
Fearless, aloof and free
Of the least breath of love or hate,
And not disconsolate
At the sick load of sorrow laid on men;
If I could keep a sanctuary there
Free even of prayer,
If I could do this, then,
With quiet candor as I grew more wise
I could look even at God with grave forgiving eyes.

1919

SPRING TORRENTS

Will it always be like this until I am dead,
   Every spring must I bear it all again
With the first red haze of the budding maple boughs,
   And the first sweet-smelling rain?

Oh I am like a rock in the rising river
   Where the flooded water breaks with a low call—
Like a rock that knows the cry of the waters
   And cannot answer at all.

1919

"LIKE BARLEY BENDING"

Like barley bending
  In low fields by the sea,
Singing in hard wind
  Ceaselessly;

Like barley bending
  And rising again,
So would I, unbroken,
  Rise from pain;

So would I softly,
  Day long, night long,
Change my sorrow
  Into song.

1919

COMPENSATION

I should be glad of loneliness
  And hours that go on broken wings,
A thirsty body, a tired heart
  And the unchanging ache of things,
If I could make a single song
  As lovely and as full of light,
As hushed and brief as a falling star
  On a winter night.

1919

"THE DREAMS OF MY HEART"

The dreams of my heart and my mind pass,
  Nothing stays with me long,
But I have had from a child
  The deep solace of song;

[63]

If that should ever leave me,
    Let me find death and stay
With things whose tunes are played out and forgotten
    Like the rain of yesterday.

1919

"WHAT DO I CARE"

What do I care, in the dreams and the languor of spring,
    That my songs do not show me at all?
For they are a fragrance, and I am a flint and a fire,
    I am an answer, they are only a call.

But what do I care, for love will be over so soon,
    Let my heart have its say and my mind stand idly by,
For my mind is proud and strong enough to be silent,
    It is my heart that makes my songs, not I.

1919

"I LOOK IN MY HEART"

I look in my heart as into a mirror
That once reflected what will not return;
The mirror is empty, I cannot bring back again
The lost faces, but I discern
Dimly my own eyes and the unsatisfied
Dark fires with which they burn.

Of the great moments, colored like jewels,
Burning and beating with triumph or pain,
Only these songs, as useless as ashes,
Only this handful of songs remain—
My heart is left like an empty mirror,
Or the ash of a fire put out by rain.

1919

1920-1926

"I AM BORNE ONWARD"

I am borne onward from the faith of my fathers,
   It is far behind me, like a fading song,
But sometimes I am homesick for its triumphant certainties,
   I who must break my heart to learn the right from the wrong.

All that I long for, shrink from or strive against,
   I must weigh in balances, frail but my own,
My fathers each one had a guardian angel,
   They leant upon them—I am alone.

                                                    1920

WHITE FOG

Heaven-invading hills are drowned
   In wide moving waves of mist,
Phlox before my door are wound
   In dripping wreaths of amethyst.

Ten feet away the solid earth
   Changes into melting cloud,
There is a hush of pain and mirth,
   No bird has heart to speak aloud.

Here in a world without a sky,
   Without the ground, without the sea,
The one unchanging thing is I,
   Myself remains to comfort me.

                                                    1920

GRAY FOG

A fog drifts in, the heavy laden
   Cold white ghost of the sea—
One by one the hills go out,
   The road and the pepper-tree.

I watch the fog float in at the window
   With the whole world gone blind,
Everything, even my longing, drowses,
   Even the thoughts in my mind.

I put my head on my hands before me,
   There is nothing left to be done or said,
There is nothing to hope for, I am tired,
   And heavy as the dead.

1920

LEISURE

If I should make no poems any more
   There would be rest at least, so let it be;
Time to read books in other tongues and listen
   To the long mellow thunder of the sea.

The year will turn for me, I shall delight in
   All animals, and some of my own kind,
Sharing with no one but myself the frosty
   And half ironic musings of my mind.

1920

"A LITTLE WHILE"

A little while when I am gone
  My life will live in music after me,
As spun foam lifted and borne on
  After the wave is lost in the full sea.

A while these nights and days will burn
  In song with the bright frailty of foam,
Living in light before they turn
  Back to the nothingness that is their home.

1920

MOONLIGHT

It will not hurt me when I am old,
  A running tide where moonlight burned
    Will not sting me like silver snakes;
The years will make me sad and cold,
  It is the happy heart that breaks.

The heart asks more than life can give,
  When that is learned, then all is learned;
    The waves break fold on jewelled fold,
But beauty itself is fugitive,
  It will not hurt me when I am old.

1920

WATER LILIES

If you have forgotten water lilies floating
    On a dark lake among mountains in the afternoon shade,
If you have forgotten their wet, sleepy fragrance,
    Then you can return and not be afraid.

But if you remember, then turn away forever
    To the plains and the prairies where pools are far apart,
There you will not come at dusk on closing water lilies,
    And the shadow of mountains will not fall on your heart.

1920

A REPLY

Four people knew the very me,
Four is enough, so let it be;
For the rest I make no chart,
There are no highroads to my heart;
The gates are locked, they will not stir
For any ardent traveller.
I have not been misunderstood,
And on the whole, I think life good—
So waste no sympathy on me
Or any well-meant gallantry;
I have enough to do to muse
On memories I would not lose.

1920

"THOSE WHO LOVE"

Those who love the most,
Do not talk of their love,
Francesca, Guinevere,
Deirdre, Iseult, Heloise,
In the fragrant gardens of heaven
Are silent, or speak if at all
Of fragile, inconsequent things.

And a woman I used to know
Who loved one man from her youth,
Against the strength of the fates
Fighting in somber pride,
Never spoke of this thing,
But hearing his name by chance,
A light would pass over her face.

1920

FACES

People that I meet and pass
   In the city's broken roar,
Faces that I lose so soon
   And have never found before,

Do you know how much you tell
   In the meeting of our eyes,
How ashamed I am, and sad
   To have pierced your poor disguise?

Secrets rushing without sound
   Crying from your hiding places—
Let me go, I cannot bear
   The sorrow of the passing faces.

—People in the restless street,
  Can it be, oh can it be
In the meeting of our eyes
  That you know as much of me?

1920

"OH YOU ARE COMING"

Oh you are coming, coming, coming,
  How will hungry Time put by the hours till then?—
But why does it anger my heart to long so
  For one man out of the world of men?

Oh I would live in myself only
  And build my life lightly and still as a dream—
Are not my thoughts clearer than your thoughts
  And colored like stones in a running stream?

Now the slow moon brightens in heaven,
  The stars are ready, the night is here—
Oh why must I lose myself to love you,
  My dear?

1920

THE SEA LOVER

I cannot be what the sea is
  To you who love the sea,
Its ease of empty spaces,
  Its soothing majesty;
To the many moods of the ocean
  Go back, for here in me
Is only its sad passion
  And changeful constancy.

1920

[74]

LOW TIDE

The birds are gathering over the dunes,
  Swerving and wheeling in shifting flight,
A thousand wings sweep darkly by
  Over the dunes and out of sight.

Why did you bring me down to the sea
  With the gathering birds and the fish-hawk flying,
The tide is low and the wind is hard,
  Nothing is left but the old year dying.

I wish I were one of the gathering birds,
  Two sharp black wings would be good for me—
When nothing is left but the old year dying,
  Why did you bring me down to the sea?

c. 1920

BLUE STARGRASS

If we took the old path
  In the old field
The same gate would stand there
  That will never yield.

Where the sun warmed us
  With a cloak made of gold,
The rain would be falling
  And the wind would be cold;

And we would stop to search
  In the wind and the rain,
But we would not find the stargrass
  By the path again.

1920

THE STORM

I thought of you when I was wakened
  By a wind that made me glad and afraid
Of the rushing, pouring sound of the sea
  That the great trees made.

One thought in my mind went over and over
  While the darkness shook and the leaves
    were thinned—
I thought it was you who had come to find me,
  You were the wind.

1920

WORDS FOR AN OLD AIR

Your heart is bound tightly, let
  Beauty beware,
It is not hers to set
  Free from the snare.

Tell her a bleeding hand
  Bound it and tied it,
Tell her the knot will stand
  Though she deride it;

One who withheld so long
  All that you yearned to take,
Has made a snare too strong
  For Beauty's self to break.

1920

UNDERSTANDING

I understood the rest too well,
And all their thoughts have come to be
Clear as grey sea-weed in the swell
Of a sunny shallow sea.

But you I never understood,
Your spirit's secret hides like gold
Sunk in a Spanish galleon
Ages ago in waters cold.

1918–20

"IF I MUST GO"

If I must go to heaven's end
Climbing the ages like a stair,
Be near me and forever bend
With the same eyes above me there;
Time will fly past us like leaves flying,
We shall not heed, for we shall be
Beyond living, beyond dying,
Knowing and known unchangeably.

1920

BROKEN THINGS

Broken things are loveliest,
Broken clouds when dusk is red,
Broken waves where a rainbow rides,
Broken words left half unsaid.

Broken things, broken things—
How quietly they comfort me,
Riven cliffs, where I can watch
The broken beauty of the sea.

1920

[77]

THE CRYSTAL GAZER

I shall gather myself into myself again,
   I shall take my scattered selves and make them one,
Fusing them into a polished crystal ball
   Where I can see the moon and the flashing sun.

I shall sit like a sibyl, hour after hour intent,
   Watching the future come and the present go,
And the little shifting pictures of people rushing
   In restless self-importance to and fro.

1921

THE SOLITARY

My heart has grown rich with the passing of years,
   I have less need now than when I was young
To share myself with every comer
   Or shape my thoughts into words with my tongue.

It is one to me that they come or go
   If I have myself and the drive of my will,
And strength to climb on a summer night
   And watch the stars swarm over the hill.

Let them think I love them more than I do,
   Let them think I care, though I go alone;
If it lifts their pride, what is it to me
   Who am self-complete as a flower or a stone.

1921

IT IS NOT I

It is not I they love
   Although they think they love me,
It is that picture of themselves they see
   As though a mirror hung above me.

I can reflect them with a grace
　　That lets them talk and makes them shine,
And if they tell their troubles to me
　　I do not bother them with mine.

It is not I they love, there is no I
　　Except for you who have me for your own,
And for the rest my heart may hide or seem
　　A thing as light as snow, as still as stone.

1921

ASHES TO ASHES

Shut your heart, though it be like a burning house,
　　Keep it shut on the shuddering cries and the roar;
There is nothing new about this fire in your heart,
　　It has all gone on for long and long before.

In the course of things it will soon be over now,
　　In a little while they will see when they go by
The light wind blowing up the winnowed ashes
　　Too white to stain the clear cold blue of the sky.

1921

SLEEPLESS NIGHT

They love me, and I have not made them happy,
　　(Rush of the wind and river whistles moaning)
They love me and I cannot give them peace,
　　(The city shifts in sleep with a low groaning).

They love me and I watch their faces aging
　　And growing pinched as the slow winter dawn;
I give them nothing but a few sad poems,
　　And life is short and we shall soon be gone.

1921

DAY'S ENDING
(Tucson)

Aloof as aged kings,
Wearing like them the purple,
The mountains ring the mesa
Crowned with a dusky light;
Many a time I watched
That coming-on of darkness
Till stars burned through the heavens
Intolerably bright.

It was not long I lived there
But I became a woman
Under those vehement stars,
For it was there I heard
For the first time my spirit
Forging an iron rule for me,
As though with slow cold hammers
Beating out word by word:

"Only yourself can heal you,
Only yourself can lead you,
The road is heavy going
And ends where no man knows;
Take love when love is given,
But never think to find it
A sure escape from sorrow
Or a complete repose."

1921

ARMOR

Men wear their pride as an armor,
　　Heavy and clanking and bright,
I too have pride for my armor
　　But I wear it hidden from sight.

[80]

The ancient kings wore shirts of mail,
  Of small links forged with such a care
That under the ermine and under the purple
  None knew that it was there.

Though the flesh was bruised till the blood dripped warm,
  Only the king alone
Knew that the blade against his breast
  Would never pierce the bone.

1921

IN THE WEB

Let be, my soul, fold your rebellious pinions,
  There is no way out of the web of things,
It is a snare that never will be broken,
  And if you struggle you will break your wings.

Be still a while, content to brood on beauty;
  Caught in the trap of space that has no end,
See how the stars, august in their submission,
  Take their Great Captor for their changeless friend.

1921

FULL MOON

(Santa Barbara)

I listened, there was not a sound to hear
  In the great rain of moonlight pouring down,
The eucalyptus trees were carved in silver,
  And a light mist of silver lulled the town.

I saw far off the grey Pacific bearing
  A broad white disk of flame,
And on the garden-walk a snail beside me
  Tracing in crystal the slow way he came.

1921

TWILIGHT

(Nahant)

There was an evening when the sky was clear,
　　Ineffably translucent in its blue;
　　The tide was falling and the sea withdrew
In hushed and happy music from the sheer
Shadowy granite of the cliffs; and fear
　　Of what life may be, and what death can do,
　　Fell from us like steel armor, and we knew
The wisdom of the Law that holds us here.
It was as though we saw the Secret Will,
　　It was as though we floated and were free;
　　　　In the south-west a planet shone serenely,
　　　　And the high moon, most reticent and queenly,
Seeing the earth had darkened and grown still,
　　Misted with light the meadows of the sea.

1921

"NOT BY THE SEA"

Not by the sea, but somewhere in the hills,
Not by the sea, but in the uplands surely
There must be rest where a dim pool demurely
Watches all night the stern slow-moving skies;

Not by the sea, that never was appeased,
Not by the sea, whose immemorial longing
Shames the tired earth where even longing dies,
Not by the sea that bore Iseult and Helen,
But in a dark green hollow of the hills
There must be sleep, even for sleepless eyes.

1921

THE WISE WOMAN

She must be rich who can forego
   An hour so jewelled with delight,
She must have treasuries of joy
   That she can draw on day and night,
She must be very sure of heaven—
   Or is it only that she feels
How much more safe it is to lack
   A thing that time so often steals.

1921

AT A PARTY

In the hot and crowded room
   Speech was roaring like the sea—
Terribly, beautifully,
   I knew you were aware of me.

Amid the bright shoulders and the black
   Of evening coats, one thing I knew—
Beautifully, terribly,
   I was aware of you.

1921

A MAN WHO UNDERSTOOD WOMEN

He meets her twice or thrice a year,
   Sometimes less and sometimes more,
Each time they meet the stage is set
   Exactly as the time before.

He is most glossy and most gay,
   Witty, omniscient, and bland,
She is inscrutable and mild,
   She lets him play his hand.

[83]

And if his pyrotechnics pale
  A little on her moonlit sky
He scarcely knows that it is so,
  And only vaguely wonders why.

And if he finds her eyes too wide,
  A shade too deep, a shade too cool,
She lets him wonder which she is,
  A saint, a sinner, or a fool.

1921

SHADOWS

We saw our shadows walking before us
  Etched on the hard sand, flat and grey,
The last thin edge of the waves crept near us,
  The autumn sunshine tried to be gay.

Chained to the shadows our bodies made there
  Slowly we walked in the dwindling light;
Our shadows faded, like wraiths we wandered
  With the dark sea booming into the night.

1921

WINTER SUN
(Lenox)

There was a bush with scarlet berries
  And there were hemlocks heaped with snow;
With a sound like surf on long sea-beaches
  They took the wind and let it go.

The hills were shining in their samite,
  Fold after fold they flowed away—
"Let come what may," your eyes were saying,
  "At least we two have had to-day."

1921

[84]

NEVER AGAIN

Never again the music blown as brightly
  Off of my heart as foam blown off a wave;
Never again the melody that lightly
  Caressed my grief and healed the wounds it gave.

Never again—I hear my dark thoughts clashing
  Sullen and blind as waves that beat a wall—
Age that is coming, summer that is going,
  All I have lost or never found at all.

1921

A JUNE DAY

I heard a red-winged black-bird singing
  Down where the river sleeps in the reeds;
That was morning, and at noontime
  A humming-bird flashed on the jewel-weeds;
Clouds blew up, and in the evening
  A yellow sunset struck through the rain,
Then blue night, and the day was ended
  That never will come again.

1921

EPITAPH

Serene descent, as a red leaf's descending
  When there is neither wind nor noise of rain,
But only autumn air and the unending
  Drawing of all things to the earth again:

So be it; let the snow sift deep and cover
  All that was drunken once with light and air;
The earth will not regret her tireless lover,
  Nor he awake to know she does not care.

1921

[85]

EFFIGY OF A NUN
(Sixteenth Century)

Infinite gentleness, infinite irony
    Are in this face with fast-sealed eyes,
And around this mouth that learned in loneliness
    How useless their wisdom is to the wise.

In her nun's habit carved, patiently, lovingly,
    By one who knew the ways of womankind,
This woman's face still keeps, in its cold wistful calm,
    All of the subtle pride of her mind.

These long patrician hands, clasping the crucifix,
    Show she had weighed the world, her will was set;
These pale curved lips of hers, holding their hidden smile,
    Once having made their choice, knew no regret.

She was of those who hoard their own thoughts carefully,
    Feeling them far too dear to give away,
Content to look at life with the high, insolent
    Air of an audience watching a play.

If she was curious, if she was passionate
    She must have told herself that love was great,
But that the lacking it might be as great a thing
    If she held fast to it, challenging fate.

She who so loved herself and her own warring thoughts,
    Watching their humorous, tragic rebound,
In her thick habit's fold, sleeping, sleeping,
    Is she amused at dreams she has found?

Infinite tenderness, infinite irony
    Are hidden forever in her closed eyes,
Who must have learned too well in her long loneliness
    How empty wisdom is, even to the wise.

1921

MOUNTAIN WATER

You have taken a drink from a wild fountain
    Early in the year;
There is nowhere to go from the top of a mountain
    But down, my dear;
And the springs that flow on the floor of the valley
    Will never seem fresh or clear
For thinking of the glitter of the mountain water
    In the feathery green of the year.   *c. 1922*

"WHEN I AM NOT WITH YOU"

When I am not with you
I am alone,
For there is no one else
And there is nothing
That comforts me but you.
When you are gone
Suddenly I am sick,
Blackness is round me,
There is nothing left.
I have tried many things,
Music and cities,
Stars in their constellations
And the sea,
But there is nothing
That comforts me but you;
And my poor pride bows down
Like grass in a rain-storm
Drenched with my longing.
The night is unbearable,
Oh let me go to you
For there is no one,
There is nothing
To comfort me but you.   *1922*

[87]

ABSENCE

I cannot sleep, the night is hot and empty,
  My thoughts leave nothing lovely in my heart,
You love me, and I love you, life is passing,
  We are apart.

The August moonlight vibrates with the voices
  Of insects and their passions frail and shrill—
Oh from what whips, oh from what secret scourgings
  All of earth's children bow before her will.

                                        1922

THE HOUR

Was it foreknown, was it foredoomed
  Before I drew my first small breath?
Will it be with me to the end,
  Will it go down with me to death?

Or was it chance, would it have been
  Another if it was not you?
Could any other voice or hands
  Have done for me what yours can do?

Now without sorrow and without elation
  I say the day I found you was foreknown,
Let the years blow like sand around that hour,
  Changeless and fixed as Memnon carved in stone.

                                        1922

THE BELOVED

It is enough of honor for one lifetime
   To have known you better than the rest have known,
The shadows and the colors of your voice,
   Your will, immutable and still as stone.

The shy heart, so lonely and so gay,
   The sad laughter and the pride of pride,
The tenderness, the depth of tenderness
   Rich as the earth, and wide as heaven is wide.

1922

AUTUMN DUSK

I saw above a sea of hills
   A solitary planet shine,
And there was no one near or far
   To keep the world from being mine.

1922

LAND'S END

The shores of the world are ours, the solitary
   Beaches that bear no fruit, nor any flowers,
Only the harsh sea-grass that the wind harries
   Hours on unbroken hours.

No one will envy us these empty reaches
   At the world's end, and none will care that we
Leave our lost footprints where the sand forever
   Takes the unchanging passion of the sea.

1922

ARCTURUS IN AUTUMN

When, in the gold October dusk, I saw you near to setting,
    Arcturus, bringer of spring,
Lord of the summer nights, leaving us now in autumn,
    Having no pity on our withering;

Oh then I knew at last that my own autumn was upon me,
    I felt it in my blood,
Restless as dwindling streams that still remember
    The music of their flood.

There in the thickening dark a wind-bent tree above me
    Loosed its last leaves in flight—
I saw you sink and vanish, pitiless Arcturus,
    You will not stay to share our lengthening night.

1922

"I SHALL LIVE TO BE OLD"

I shall live to be old, who feared I should die young,
    I shall live to be old.
I shall cling to life as the leaves to the creaking oak
    In the rustle of falling snow and the cold.

The other trees let loose their leaves on the air
    In their russet and red,
I have lived long enough to wonder which is the best,
    And to envy sometimes the way of the early dead.

1922

WINTER

I shall have winter now and lessening days,
Lit by a smoky sun with slanting rays,
And after falling leaves, the first determined frost.
The colors of the world will all be lost.
So be it; the faint buzzing of the snow

[90]

Will fill the empty boughs,
And after sleet storms I shall wake to see
A glittering glassy plume of every tree.
Nothing shall tempt me from my fire-lit house.
And I shall find at night a friendly ember
And make my life of what I can remember.

1922

WINTER NIGHT SONG

Will you come as of old with singing,
    And shall I hear as of old?
Shall I rush to open the window
    In spite of the arrowy cold?

        Ah no, my dear, ah no,
            I shall sit by the fire reading,
        Though you sing half the night in the snow
            I shall not be heeding.

Though your voice remembers the forest,
    The warm green light and the birds,
Though you gather the sea in your singing
    And pour its sound into words,

        Even so, my dear, even so,
            I shall not heed you at all;
        Though your shoulders are white with snow,
            Though you strain your voice to a call,
        I shall drowse and the fire will drowse,
            The draught will be cold on the floor,
        The clock running down,
            Snow banking the door.

c. 1922

WISDOM

It was a night of early spring,
  The winter-sleep was scarcely broken;
Around us shadows and the wind
  Listened for what was never spoken.

Though half a score of years are gone,
  Spring comes as sharply now as then—
But if we had it all to do
  It would be done the same again.

It was a spring that never came,
  But we have lived enough to know
What we have never had, remains;
  It is the things we have that go.

                                    1922

HIDE AND SEEK

When I was a child we played sometimes in the dark;
  Hide and seek in the dark is a terrible game,
With the nerves pulled tight in fear of the stealthy seeker,
  With the brief exultance, and the blood in the veins like flame.

Now I see that life is a game in the dark,
  A groping in shadows, a brief exultance, a dread
Of what may crouch beside us or lurk behind us,
  A leaving of what we want to say unsaid,
Sure of one thing only, a long sleep
When the game is over and we are put to bed.

                                    1922

"I HAVE SEEN THE SPRING"

Nothing is new, I have seen the spring too often;
There have been other plum-trees white as this one
Like a silvery cloud tethered beside the road,

I have been waked from sleep too many times
By birds at dawn boasting their love is beautiful.
The grass-blades gleam in the wind, nothing is changed.
Nothing is lost, it is all as it used to be,
Unopened lilacs are still as deep a purple,
The boughs of the elm are dancing still in a veil of tiny leaves,
Nothing is lost but a few years from my life.   *c. 1922*

MARCH NIGHTS

The thin night wind is cold,
And the stars that rise with spring,
Vega, Arcturus, Spica,
Are sharp in their changeless youth,

The scarcely budded trees
Give themselves up to the wind,
There is never a shelter here
From the stars and the scent of the earth.

Too late, too late, too late,
Nothing could come or go
That would not be too late—
I have borne too many springs.   *1922*

AN END

I have no heart for any other joy,
    The drenched September day turns to depart,
And I have said good-bye to what I love;
    With my own will I vanquished my own heart.

On the long wind I hear the winter coming,
    The window panes are cold and blind with rain;
With my own will I turned the summer from me
    And summer will not come to me again.
                              c. 1922

[93]

THE OLD ENEMY

Rebellion against death, the old rebellion
  Is over; I have nothing left to fight;
Battles have always had their meed of music
  But peace is quiet as a windless night.

Therefore I make no songs—I have grown certain
  Save when he comes too late, death is a friend,
A shepherd leading home his flock serenely
  Under the planet at the evening's end.

                                    1922

SAND DRIFT

I thought I should not walk these dunes again,
  Nor feel the sting of this wind-bitten sand,
Where the coarse grasses always blow one way,
  Bent, as my thoughts are, by an unseen hand.

I have returned; where the last wave rushed up
  The wet sand is a mirror for the sky
A bright blue instant, and along its sheen
  The nimble sandpipers run twinkling by.

Nothing has changed; with the same hollow thunder
  The waves die in their everlasting snow—
Only the place we sat is drifted over,
  Lost in the blowing sand, long, long ago.

                                c. 1922

FOREKNOWN

They brought me with a secret glee
   The news I knew before they spoke,
      And though they hoped to see me riven,
      They found me light as dry leaves driven
   Before the storm that splits an oak.

For I had learned from many an autumn
   The way a leaf can drift and go,
      Lightly, lightly, almost gay
      Taking the unreturning way
   To mix with winter and the snow.

1923

"SHE WHO COULD BIND YOU"

She who could bind you
   Could bind fire to a wall;
She who could hold you
   Could hold a waterfall;
She who could keep you
   Could keep the wind from blowing
On a warm spring night
   With a low moon glowing.

1923

[95]

THE FLIGHT

We are two eagles
Flying together
Under the heavens,
Over the mountains,
Stretched on the wind.
Sunlight heartens us,
Blind snow baffles us,
Clouds wheel after us
Ravelled and thinned.

We are like eagles,
But when Death harries us,
Human and humbled
When one of us goes,
Let the other follow,
Let the flight be ended,
Let the fire blacken,
Let the book close.

1923

OVERHEARD

You are the only one
Who has ever known
The wild beat of that heart,
The slow drip of its blood
From a wound that will not heal.
You are the only one
Who will ever know.

Life is a strong thing,
It gives way slowly;
Love is a strong thing
And the years are strong.
Where these struggle together
The blood drips softly,
And since they are evenly matched
The fight is long.

                                    1923

AUTUMN SONG

Turn, turn away, gather no more of the holly,
  Winter has not yet come, though the sun in the south is low
And the wind has the twang of a harp whose player is over-eager—
  Gather the red leaves now and let the holly go.

Gather as fast as you can the crimson, the bronze, the yellow,
  You are tall, reach higher up while I take the ones below,
I am afraid of winter—the thorns of the holly hurt me—
  We can gather it if we must after a fall of snow.

                                    1923

"I COULD SNATCH A DAY"

I could snatch a day out of the late autumn
  And set it trembling like forgotten springs,
There would be sharp blue skies with new leaves shining
  And flying shadows cast by flying wings.

I could take the heavy wheel of the world and break it,
  But we sit brooding while the ashes fall,
Cowering over an old fire that dwindles,
  Waiting for nothing at all.

                                    1923

[97]

"COOL AS THE TOUCH OF A STONE"

Cool as the touch of a stone,
　　Gentle as falling snow,
So let your thoughts seem,
　　So let your words flow.

Let your harp stand untouched
　　With all its slackened wires,
Sing for yourself alone
　　Of the dark, sleepless fires.

1923

AFTER MIDNIGHT, LONDON

Over the melancholy sea of roofs
With skylights pricked to silver in the moonlight,
Over the hollow streets, patient, deserted,
With glaring lamps, shedding their light for no one;
Over it all I look from my high window,
Sleepless, an alien in this ancient city,
Aware of all the seven million souls
Asleep or wanting sleep under these roofs—
Aware at last how little a thing my life is,—
If I am useless, if I am unhappy
It is of small concern even to me,
And no concern at all to all these others.

1923

ON THE SUSSEX DOWNS

Over the downs there were birds flying,
　　Far off glittered the sea,
And toward the north the weald of Sussex
　　Lay like a kingdom under me.

I was happier than the larks
    That nest on the downs and sing to the sky,
Over the downs the birds flying
    Were not so happy as I.

It was not you, though you were near,
    Though you were good to hear and see,
It was not earth, it was not heaven
    It was myself that sang in me.

                                    c. 1923

IN THE WOOD

I heard the water-fall rejoice
    Singing like a choir,
I saw the sun flash out of it
    Azure and amber fire.

The earth was like an open flower
    Enamelled and arrayed,
The path I took to find its heart
    Fluttered with sun and shade.

And while earth lured me, gently, gently,
    Happy and all alone,
Suddenly a heavy snake
    Reared black upon a stone.

                                    1923

THE TUNE

I know a certain tune that my life plays;
    Over and over I have heard it start
With all the wavering loveliness of viols
    And gain in swiftness like a runner's heart.

It climbs and climbs; I watch it sway in climbing
  High over time, high even over doubt,
It has all heaven to itself—it pauses
  And faltering blindly down the air, goes out.

                                        1923

"THERE WILL BE STARS"

There will be stars over the place forever;
  Though the house we loved and the street we loved are lost,
Every time the earth circles her orbit
  On the night the autumn equinox is crossed,
Two stars we knew, poised on the peak of midnight
  Will reach their zenith; stillness will be deep;
There will be stars over the place forever,
  There will be stars forever, while we sleep.

                                        1923

"EGYPTIAN KINGS WERE BURIED"

        Egyptian kings were buried
          With all their golden gear,
        Cup and chest and chariot,
          Couch and battle-spear.

        Centuries of solid night
          Pass them as an hour goes by;
        When the chamber is unsealed
          The gold looks gayly at the sky.

        But the kingly body lies
          Like a bit of blackened leather;
        All the wrappings round the king
          Cannot hold his bones together.

All the unguents and the spice,
    All the power of pride or tears
Cannot keep the human body
    Past its few small years.

                                1923

THE HAWK

Men have tried to be kind,
    But life is a hard thing,
And the hawk is always above us,
    Black hawk with a wide wing,
Swift, with a sharp eye
    Against the indifferent sky.

We scurry and huddle beneath,
    Driven always two ways
By the two quarrelling shepherds
    The Flesh and the Mind—
There is dust and dark wind
    And the hawk sweeps down and slays.

                                1924

"LET IT BE YOU"

Let it be you who lean above me
    On my last day,
Let it be you who shut my eyelids
    Forever and aye.

Say a "Good-night" as you have said it
    All of these years,
With the old look, with the old whisper
    And without tears.

You will know then all that in silence
   You always knew,
Though I have loved, I loved no other
   As I love you.

1924

SEPTEMBER NIGHT

We walked in the dew, in the drowsy starlight
   To the sleepless, sleepy sound
Of insects singing in the low sea-meadows
   For miles and miles around;
With a wheel and a whirr the resistless rhythm
   Trembled incessantly;
Antares was red in the sky before us,
   And behind us, the blackness of the sea.

c. 1924

TO A SEA GULL IN THE CITY

On level and illumined wings, high over
   Our discontent, you circle in the cold
Uncolored sky; the meager winter sunlight
   Lays on your wings its oily flakes of gold.

Above our noise, our broken loves, our barter,
   You move in lonely and serene delight—
The tears that could not fall for my own sorrow
   Have blessed the eyes that lift to watch your flight.

1924

"SO THIS WAS ALL"

So this was all there was to the great play
    She had come so far to act in, this was all—
    Except the short last scene and the slow fall
Of the final curtain, that might catch half-way,
As final curtains do, and leave the grey
    Lorn end of things too long exposed. The hall
    Clapped faintly, and she took her curtain call,
Knowing how little she had left to say.
And in the pause before the last act started,
    Slowly unpinning the roses she had worn,
        She reconsidered lines that had been said,
And found them hardly worthy the high-hearted
    Ardor that she had brought, nor the bright, torn
        Roses that shattered round her, dripping red.

c. 1924

LATE OCTOBER
(Bois de Boulogne)

Listen, the damp leaves on the walks are blowing
    With a ghost of sound;
Is it a fog or is it a rain dripping
    From the low trees to the ground?

If I had gone before, I could have remembered
    Lilacs and green after-noons of May;
I chose to wait, I chose to hear from autumn
    Whatever she has to say.

1924

FONTAINEBLEAU

Interminable palaces front on the green parterres,
 And ghosts of ladies lovely and immoral
Glide down the gilded stairs,
 The high cold corridors are clicking with the heel taps
That long ago were theirs.

But in the sunshine, in the vague autumn sunshine,
 The geometric gardens are desolately gay;
The crimson and scarlet and rose-red dahlias
 Are painted like the ladies who used to pass this way
With a ringletted monarch, a Henry or a Louis
 On a lost October day.

The aisles of the garden lead into the forest,
 The aisles lead into autumn, a damp wind grieves,
Ghostly kings are hunting, the boar breaks cover,
 But the sounds of horse and horn are hushed in falling
  leaves,
 Four centuries of autumns, four centuries of leaves.

1924

AUTUMN

(Parc Monceau)

I shall remember only these leaves falling
 Small and incessant in the still air,
Yellow leaves on the dark green water resting
 And the marble Venus there—
Is she pointing to her breasts or trying to hide them?
 There is no god to care.

The colonnade curves close to the leaf-strewn water
 And its reflection seems
Lost in the mass of leaves and unavailing
 As a dream lost among dreams;
The colonnade curves close to the leaf-strewn water
 A dream lost among dreams.

1924

SEPTEMBER DAY

(Pont de Neuilly)

The Seine flows out of the mist
  And into the mist again;
The trees lean over the water,
  The small leaves fall like rain.

The leaves fall patiently,
  Nothing remembers or grieves;
The river takes to the sea
  The yellow drift of the leaves.

Milky and cold is the air,
  The leaves float with the stream,
The river comes out of a sleep
  And goes away in a dream.

1924

"I LIVED IN MY LIFE AS A DREAM"

I lived in my life as a dream,
The unrest, the haste unending,
Were as the unrest of a dream,
The search was a search in a dream.
But I said, "When I go home
To the house we have known together
I shall tear myself out of this web
Of spidery silver.
The man's voice that waked me
(If ever I was awakened),
I can call to mind in that house . . ."
But when I had opened the door,
When I stood again in that room
It was empty,
I could not recall
The way his voice lived and its low

[105]

Beating and violent beauty.
I only knew it was lovely—I could not remember its ways.

The chairs, the curtains, the cushions
That had lived in that river of sound
So many and many a night,
That were saturated with sound
Of the voice that I tried to hear,
Left me still in the stillness.
Then I cried to my mind
"Call it back! Is memory nothing at all
But a place to lose one's treasures?"
Yet only the dusty voices
Of many another came calling
In a thin confusion and clamor—
The voice that I loved was not there;
I remembered all it had seemed like,
I could not capture itself.
I said, "It is peaceful as mountains
Vague and great in the moonlight;
It is clear as the word
Of a cow-bell far off through the soft rain
In a place of moist fragrance and foliage;
It is heavy as the eternal
Unanswered questions of man;
Insistent as the sudden
Call of a plucked violin string"—
Ugh—these are words, I shall be
Beseeching my brain no more.
Let that sound be lost in my heart—
Let me live out my life as a dream.

1925

CLEAR EVENING

The crescent moon is large enough to linger
  A little while after the twilight goes,
This moist midsummer night the garden perfumes
  Are earth and apple, dewy pine and rose.

Over my head four new-cut stars are glinting
  And the inevitable night draws on;
I am alone, the old terror takes me,
  Evenings will come like this when I am gone;

Evenings on evenings, years on years forever—
  Be taut, my spirit, close upon and keep
The scent, the brooding chill, the gliding fire-fly,
  A poem learned before I fall asleep.

                                      1925

"BEAUTIFUL, PROUD SEA"

Careless forever, beautiful proud sea,
  You laugh in happy thunder all alone,
You fold upon yourself, you dance your dance
  Impartially on drift-weed, sand or stone.

You make us believe that we can outlive death,
  You make us for an instant, for your sake,
Burn, like stretched silver of a wave,
  Not breaking, but about to break.

                                      1925

CONFLICT

The Spartan and the Sybarite
Battle in me day and night;
Evenly matched, relentless, wary,
Each one cursing his adversary,
With my slow blood dripping wet
They fight from sunrise to sunset.
And from sunset the fight goes on,
I shiver and hear them in the dawn;
They fight to the death this time, but I
Care little which will have to die,
Whichever it is, when the end has come,
I shall be the defeated one.

1925

[FEEL MY SILENCE SPEAK]

Feel my silence speak,
    And my hands that do not move
Hurt you with the hot
    Hurry of their love.

A stone is not more still,
    Nor the hearth-cat more tame,—
Yet the stone was formed in fire
    And the cat from the tiger came.

1925

AUGUST NIGHT

On a midsummer night, on a night that was eerie with stars,
  In a wood too deep for a single star to look through,
You led down a path whose turnings you knew in the
      darkness,
  But the scent of the dew-dripping cedars was all that I knew.

I drank of the darkness, I was fed with the honey of fragrance,
  I was glad of my life, the drawing of breath was sweet;
I heard your voice, you said, "Look down, see the glow-worm!"
  It was there before me, a small star white at my feet.

We watched while it brightened as though it were breathed
      on and burning,
  This tiny creature moving over earth's floor—
" 'L'amor che move il sole e l'altre stelle,' "
  You said, and no more.

                                        1925

TWO MINDS

  Your mind and mine are such great lovers they
  Have freed themselves from cautious human clay,
  And on wild clouds of thought, naked together
  They ride above us in extreme delight;
  We see them, we look up with a lone envy
  And watch them in their zone of crystal weather
  That changes not for winter or the night.

                                    1925

APPRAISAL

Never think she loves him wholly,
Never believe her love is blind,
All his faults are locked securely
In a closet of her mind;
All his indecisions folded
Like old flags that time has faded,
Limp and streaked with rain,
And his cautiousness like garments
Frayed and thin, with many a stain—
Let them be, oh let them be,
There is treasure to outweigh them,
His proud will that sharply stirred,
Climbs as surely as the tide,
Senses strained too taut to sleep,
Gentleness to beast and bird,
Humor flickering hushed and wide
As the moon on moving water,
And a tenderness too deep
To be gathered in a word.

1925

TO A LOOSE WOMAN

My dear, your face is lovely,
    And you have lovely eyes,
I do not cavil at your life,
    But only at your lies—
You are not brave, you are not wild,
    You merely ride the crest of fashion;
Ambition is your special ware
    And you have dared to call it passion.

1926

THIS HAND

Must I watch this hand grow old,
   Till the skin slacken and wrinkle and shine,
The comely shape and color gone,
   And yet the hand be mine?

The oak tree drops its leaves unknowing,
   And heedless drifts away the rose—
We hoard our prime, we dread its going
   And watch it while it goes.

1926

SECRET TREASURE

Fear not that my music seems
Like water locked in winter streams;
You are the sun that many a time
Thawed those rivers into rhyme,
But let them for a while remain
A hidden music in my brain.

Unmeaning phrase and wordless measure,
That unencumbered loveliness
Which is a poet's secret treasure
Sings in me now, and sings no less
That even for your lenient eyes
It will not live in written guise.

1926

THE FOUNTAIN

Fountain, fountain, what do you say
   Singing at night alone?
"It is enough to rise and fall
   Here in my basin of stone."

But are you content as you seem to be
So near the freedom and rush of the sea?
   "I have listened all night to its laboring sound,
   It heaves and sags, as the moon runs round;
Ocean and fountain, shadow and tree,
Nothing escapes, nothing is free."

1926

ON A MARCH DAY

Here in the teeth of this triumphant wind
   That shakes the naked shadows on the ground,
Making a key-board of the earth to strike
   From clattering tree and hedge a separate sound,

Bear witness for me that I loved my life,
   All things that hurt me and all things that healed,
And that I swore to it this day in March,
   Here at the edge of this new-broken field.

You only knew me, tell them I was glad
   For every hour since my hour of birth,
And that I ceased to fear, as once I feared,
   The last complete reunion with the earth.

1926

AUTUMN ON THE BEACHES

Not more blue at the dawn of the world,
　　Not more virgin or more gay,
Never in all the million years
　　Was the sea happier than to-day.

The sand was not more trackless then,
　　Morning more stainless or more cold—
Only the forest and the fields
　　Know that the year is old.

1926

LINES

These are the ultimate highlands,
Like chord on chord of music
Climbing to rest
On the highest peak and the bluest
Large on the luminous heavens
Deep in the west.

1926

1927-1932

1922-1932

AGE

Brooks sing in the spring
   And in summer cease;
I who sang in my youth
   Now hold my peace;
Youth is a noisy stream
   Chattering over the ground,
But the sad wisdom of age
   Wells up without sound.

c. 1927

[LET NEVER MUSIC SOUND]

Let never music sound
   Unless an angel make it;
Let stillness reign around
   Until a seraph break it—
No song was ever noble
   As the unsullied wide
Prairies of silence sleeping
   In peace on every side.

1927

"ALL THAT WAS MORTAL"

All that was mortal shall be burned away,
   All that was mind shall have been put to sleep.
Only the spirit shall awake to say
   What the deep says to the deep;
But for an instant, for it too is fleeting—
   As on a field with new snow everywhere,
Footprints of birds record a brief alighting
   In flight begun and ended in the air.

1927

[117]

"THERE WILL BE REST"

There will be rest, and sure stars shining
  Over the roof-tops crowned with snow,
A reign of rest, serene forgetting,
  The music of stillness holy and low.

I will make this world of my devising
  Out of a dream in my lonely mind,
I shall find the crystal of peace,—above me
  Stars I shall find.

c. 1927

CALM MORNING AT SEA

Midocean like a pale blue morning-glory
  Opened wide, wide:
The ship cut softly through the silken surface;
  We watched white sea-birds ride
Unrocking on the holy virgin water
  Fleckless on every side.

1927

MOONLIGHT ON THE BED

No moon would rise till after midnight,
  And yet this light was plain;
It seemed to the heavy silver of moonlight
  As dew is to rain.

I lifted my head, from the window westward
  All I could see
Was the grave splendor of a single planet
  Opposite me.

1928

MOON'S ENDING

Moon, worn thin to the width of a quill,
  In the dawn clouds flying,
How good to go, light into light, and still
  Giving light, dying.

1928

THE FALLING STAR

I saw a star slide down the sky,
Blinding the north as it went by,
Too burning and too quick to hold,
Too lovely to be bought or sold,
Good only to make wishes on
And then forever to be gone.

1929

[OH YES, MY DEAR, OH YES]

Oh yes, my dear, oh yes,
There is flint in me,
There is stone.
Were you blind, could you never guess,
Had you never known?
Could you not, long since, have foretold
In the dark and alone
There would flash an edge of fire
When flint struck stone?

1929

ON HELTON'S HILL

(The Berkshires)

There is no other hill
  The whole earth over
That shows so wide a world
  Or smells so sweet of clover;

Three tiers of hills, the green,
  The silver green, the blue,
And farms in every valley
  With harvest gathered new.

The sun at pride of noon
  With all his light to give—
World, I have loved you well,
  I am glad to live.
                                1930

CHANGE

Change, in a world of change, follows me even here;
This broken curve of the dune is not as it was last year,
Sea-grass grows sparser now where the east wind whips and
    turns,
And low in the yellow west a different planet burns.
                                1931

IN A DARKENING GARDEN

Gather together, against the coming of night,
  All that we played with here,
Toys and fruits, the quill from the sea-bird's flight,
  The small flute, hollow and clear;
The apple that was not eaten, the grapes untasted—
  Let them be put away.
They served for us, I would not have them wasted,
  They lasted out our day.
                                1931

[120]

LAST PRELUDE

If this shall be the last time
The melody flies upward
With its rush of sparks in flight,
Let me go up with it in fire and laughter,
Or let me drown if need be
Lost in the swirl of light.
The violins are tuning, whimpering, catching thunder
From the suppressed dark agony of viols—
Once more let heaven clutch me, plunge me under
Miles on uncounted miles.

1931

GRACE BEFORE SLEEP

How can our minds and bodies be
Grateful enough that we have spent
Here in this generous room, we three,
This evening of content?
Each one of us has walked through storm
And fled the wolves along the road;
But here the hearth is wide and warm,
And for this shelter and this light
Accept, O Lord, our thanks to-night.

1931

WISDOM

Oh to relinquish, with no more of sound
Than the bent bough's when the bright apples fall;
Oh to let go, without a cry or call
That can be heard by any above ground;
Let the dead know, but not the living see—
The dead who loved me will not suffer, knowing
It is all one, the coming or the going,
If I have kept the last, essential me.
If that is safe, then I am safe indeed,

[121]

It is my citadel, my church, my home,
My mother and my child, my constant friend;
It is my music, making for my need
A pæan like the cymbals of the foam,
Or silence, level, spacious, without end.
                                    1931

[YOUR FACE IS BEAUTIFUL BEYOND
ALL OTHER FACES]

Your face is beautiful beyond all other faces;
Beyond all music and all poetry
Your face is beautiful to me.
I am reminded always of sea beaches
That lately have been laved with storm
And have no more to show
Now to the searcher than one shell, like snow,
Fluted more deep than shallow-water shells—
Your face is beautiful beyond all other faces,
More to me now than dear remembered places,
More to me now than anything I know.
                                    1931

ADVICE TO A GIRL

No one worth possessing
Can be quite possessed;
Lay that on your heart,
My young angry dear;
This truth, this hard and precious stone,
Lay it on your hot cheek,
Let it hide your tear.
Hold it like a crystal
When you are alone
And gaze in the depths of the icy stone.
Long, look long and you will be blessed:
No one worth possessing
Can be quite possessed.
                                    1931

[122]

TO A CHILD WATCHING THE GULLS

(Queenstown Harbor)

The painted light was on their underwings,
    And on their firm curved breasts the painted light,
Sailing they swerved in the red air of sunset
    With petulant cries unworthy of their flight;
But on their underwings that fleeting splendor,
    Those chilly breasts an instant burning red—
You who are young, O you who will outlive me,
    Remember them for the indifferent dead.

        1931

"SINCE DEATH BRUSHED PAST ME"

Since Death brushed past me once more to-day,
Let me say quickly what I must say:
Take without shame the love I give you,
Take it before I am hurried away.

You are intrepid, noble, kind,
My heart goes to you with my mind,
The plummet of your thought is long
Sunk in deep water, cold with song.
You are all I asked, my dear—
My words are said, my way is clear.

        1931

TO THE SEA

Bitter and beautiful, sing no more;
Scarf of spindrift strewn on the shore,
Burn no more in the noon-day light,
Let there be night for me, let there be night.

On the restless beaches I used to range
The two that I loved have walked with me—
I saw them change and my own heart change—
I cannot face the unchanging sea.

        1931

[123]

[SHE WENT BEFORE THE NIGHT CAME DOWN]

She went before the night came down,
But she left candles lit,
A young fire playing on the hearth,
A peaceful chair drawn close to it,
Something to eat upon the plate,
And books upon the shelf—
Everything as it always was
Except that simple thing, herself.

1931

ASHES

Laid in a quiet corner of the world
There will be left no more of me some night
Than the lone bat could carry in his flight
Over the meadows when the moon is furled;
I shall be then so little, and so lost,
Only the many-fingered rain will find me,
And I have taken thought to leave behind me
Nothing to feel the long on-coming frost.

Now without sorrow and without elation
I can lay down my body, nor deplore
How little, with her insufficient ration,
Life has to feed us—but these hands, must they
Go in the same blank, ignominious way,
And fold upon themselves, at last, no more?

1931

STRANGE VICTORY

To this, to this, after my hope was lost,
    To this strange victory;
To find you with the living, not the dead,
    To find you glad of me;
To find you wounded even less than I,
    Moving as I across the stricken plain;
After the battle to have found your voice
    Lifted above the slain.

1931

TRUCE

Take heart, for now the battle is half over,
    We have not shamed our sires;
Pride, the lone pennon, ravelled by the storm-wind
    Stands in the sunset fires.

It may be, with the coming-on of evening
    We shall be granted unassailed repose,
And what is left of dusk will be less darkness
    Than luminous air, on which the crescent glows.

1931

IN MEMORY OF VACHEL LINDSAY

"Deep in the ages," you said, "deep in the ages,"
    And, "To live in mankind is far more than to live in a name."
You are deep in the ages, now, deep in the ages,
    You whom the world could not break, nor the years tame.

Fly out, fly on, eagle that is not forgotten,
    Fly straight to the innermost light, you who loved sun in
        your eyes,
Free of the fret, free of the weight of living,
    Bravest among the brave, gayest among the wise.

1931

[125]

FROM A HIGH WINDOW

(New York, December, 1931)

From a high window, this December night,
The spangled city, tremulously gay,
Cried out to us from every amber light:
"Oh love me, love me, for I cannot stay;
My forehead leans too close against the stars,
I am the tallest city of all time,
But I shall be the prey of little wars,
I shall go down to heaps of rust and lime.
I am a princess, lithe and swaying lightly
Above the housewife cities of the earth;
I shall reward you not, but love me nightly
Though I shall bring no race of men to birth;
Oh love me, praise me, fold me in your song—
Though I am lovely, I am not for long."

1931

RETURN TO A COUNTRY HOUSE

Nothing but darkness enters in this room,
Nothing but darkness and the winter night,
Yet on this bed once years ago a light
Silvered the sheets with an unearthly bloom;
It was the planet Venus in the west
Casting a square of brightness on this bed,
And in that light your dark and lovely head
Lay for a while and seemed to be at rest.
But that the light is gone, and that no more
Even if it were here, would you be here,—
That is one line in a long tragic play
That has been acted many times before,
And acted best when not a single tear
Falls,—when the mind and not the heart holds sway.

1932

EVEN TO-DAY

What if the bridge men built goes down,
What if the torrent sweeps the town,
The hills are safe, the hills remain,
And hills are happy in the rain;
If I can climb the hills and find
A small square cottage to my mind,
A lonely but a cleanly house
With shelves too bare to tempt a mouse,
Whatever years remain to me
I shall live out in dignity.

1932

TO M.

Till the last sleep, from the blind waking at birth,
    Bearing the weight of the years between the two,
I shall find no better thing upon the earth
    Than the wilful, noble, faulty thing which is you.

You have not failed me; but if you too should fail me,
    Being human, bound on your own inviolate quest,
No matter now what the years do to assail me
    I shall go, in some sort, a victor, down to my rest.

1932

Appendix

Previously unpublished poems, from manuscripts in the Beinecke Rare Book and Manuscript Library, Yale University:

Poems selected from individual volumes but not included in *The Collected Poems of Sara Teasdale* (1937):

Texts of poems published by Sara Teasdale; see manuscript versions, pp. 37 and 43:

SONG MAKING

My heart cried like a beaten child
    Ceaselessly all night long;
I had to take my own cries
    And thread them into a song.

One was a cry at black midnight
    And one when the first cock crew—
My heart was like a beaten child,
    But no one ever knew.

Life, you have put me in your debt
    And I must serve you long—
But oh, the debt is terrible
    That must be paid in song.

1916

[131]

"ONLY IN SLEEP"

Only in sleep I see their faces,
    Children I played with when I was a child,
Louise comes back with her brown hair braided,
    Annie with ringlets warm and wild.

Only in sleep Time is forgotten—
    What may have come to them, who can know?
    Yet we played last night as long ago,
And the doll-house stood at the turn of the stair.

The years had not sharpened their smooth round faces,
    I met their eyes and found them mild—
Do they, too, dream of me, I wonder,
    And for them am I, too, a child?

1918

Index to First Lines

[133]

Gather together, against the coming of night	120
Gray pilgrim, you have journeyed far	4
He meets her twice or thrice a year	83
Heaven-invading hills are drowned	69
Here in the teeth of this triumphant wind	112
Hibiscus flowers are cups of fire	44
How can our minds and bodies be	121
How many million Aprils came	48
Hushed in the smoky haze of summer sunset	38
I am a wave that cannot reach the land	9
I am alone, in spite of love	42
I am borne onward from the faith of my fathers	69
I am not yours, not lost in you	22
I asked the heaven of stars	10
I built a little House of Dreams	3
I came from the sunny valleys	9
I came to the crowded Inn of Earth	7
I cannot be what the sea is	74
I cannot die, who drank delight	39
I cannot sleep, the night is hot and empty	88
I could snatch a day out of the late autumn	97
I do not love you now	28
I gave my life to another lover	21
I have no heart for any other joy	93
I have no riches but my thoughts	31
I heard a cry in the night	6
I heard a red-winged black-bird singing	85
I heard a wood thrush in the dusk	32
I heard the water-fall rejoice	99
I hoped that he would love me	4
I knew you thought of me all night	40
I know a certain tune that my life plays	99
I lift my heart as spring lifts up	12
I like to think of you among still mountains	51
I listened, there was not a sound to hear	81
I lived in my life as a dream	105
I look in my heart as into a mirror	64
I love my hour of wind and light	16

[137]